Smart Play

Smart Play

101 Fun, Easy Games That Enhance Intelligence

BARBARA SHER

ILLUSTRATIONS BY
RALPH BUTLER

WILEY

JOHN WILEY & SONS, INC.

Published by John Wiley & Sons, Inc., Hoboken, New Jersey
Published simultaneously in Canada

Design and production by Navta Associates, Inc.

The publisher and the author have made every reasonable effort to insure that the experiments and activities in this book are safe when conducted as instructed but assume no responsibility for any damage caused or sustained while performing the experiments or activities in this book. Parent, guardians, and/or teachers should supervise young readers who undertake the experiments and activities in this book.

For general information about our other products and services, please contact our Customer Care Department within the United States at (800) 762-2974, outside the United States at (317) 572-3993 or fax (317) 572-4002.

Wiley also publishes its books in a variety of electronic formats. Some content that appears in print may not be available in electronic books. For more information about Wiley products, visit our web site at www.wiley.com.

Library of Congress Cataloging-in-Publication Data
Sher, Barbara.
    Smart play : 101 fun, easy games that enhance intelligence / Barbara Sher ;
   illustrations by Ralph Butler.
       p.   cm.
   Includes index.
   ISBN 0-471-46673-5 (pbk. : alk. paper)
    1. Educational games. 2. Family recreation. I. Title.
  GV1480.S54 2004
  371.33'7—dc22

                                                      2004002247

Printed in the United States of America

10 9 8 7 6 5 4 3 2 1

This book is dedicated to all the wonderful children everywhere who have played these games with me, especially to my young playmates on the islands of Saipan, Tinian, and Rota.

Contents ⌄ ⌄ ⌄ ⌄ ⌄ ⌄ ⌄ ⌄ ⌄ ⌄ ⌄ ⌄

PART FOUR   Games That Enhance Kinesthetic Skills   99

` ´ ` ´
PART FIVE

Games That Enhance Interpersonal Skills   147

Index   177

Acknowledgments

People often ask me how long it takes to write my books. I answer that each book takes about a year to write, and about thirty years to gather the materials to write about.

If I wanted to be even more accurate, I'd probably say sixty years, because getting the confidence to write a book took the love and unconditional support from my family of birth and the family I made; it took encouragement from my loving friends and the enthusiastic response from the teachers at the schools and the participants at the national and international workshops I have given. Especially, it took the lessons I got from my main teachers: the children who have played all of these games with me. They have had a harsh but honest approach that lets me know which games work and which don't. They either respond with excitement or they just wander away. The games in this book have been well field-tested and only the most successful ones made the grade.

My books are also always inspired by my wonderful daughters. They have been my creative assistants at international workshops, my first readers, my game players, my emotional support, and my friends. I'll never stop appreciating the presence (and present) of Marissa, Roxanne, and Jessica. For my dear friend Jenny Slack who gave me love and clear thoughts during the rewriting phase, and my good pal and colleague Patty Staal who enthusiastically plays these games with me at the schools, I also give thanks.

Of course, it's one thing to write a book and quite another to get it to you. For this, I owe big thanks to my great agent, Judi Schuler, who is quick to answer my e-mail and fulfill my needs. I owe gratitude to my former editor, Carole Hall, who said she thought of me as an "unending diamond mine" of ideas. I owe appreciation to my present editor, Kate Bradford, who has a keen editing eye and plays games with her own children. I am grateful to my delightful illustrator Ralph Butler, who made the drawings exactly as I want them, and to the people at John Wiley & Sons, especially John Simko, who does the difficult legwork of turning a manuscript into a book.

Most important, I want to acknowledge you, my readers, for taking my ideas and using them with the children you care for. It is this step that takes the love that is behind my words and spreads it out into the world. Thank you, thank you, thank you.

Introduction

Lessons learned through our bodies stick with us. We don't read a manual to learn how to ride a bike or play a game of Ping-Pong. We learn through our bodies, and once our bodies learn something, we never forget it.

This same kind of body intelligence can be used to help children learn their mental skills. Children will have more of an internal awareness of what *5* means by jumping forward five times in a Mother-May-I game than by looking at a picture of five rabbits.

Children who play the game of making the letter *A* using their fingers are going to remember how to form that letter faster than if they just see it written.

Children who get to mime the words *sweatpants* and *dragonfly* for others to guess are never going to forget what compound words are.

Children who move their bodies as part of the learning process are stimulated and alert. They also increase their body coordination, and learning to move one's body well is important whether one chooses to climb a mountain or dance the latest steps or just walk down the road with style and grace.

To promote using movement and fun as a way to increase cognitive and kinesthetic learning, I have given workshops in such varied places as orphanages in Cambodia, colleges in New Zealand, and schools in Nicaragua and Micronesia. I show caregivers, parents, teachers, and children fun ways to play that enhance their intelligence.

There are two major reasons why I'm serious about fun.

First, research shows that anything learned with tension often gets flushed out along with the unpleasant memories.

Second, the fun factor lifts our spirits and gives us that sense of well-being that opens our minds and hearts. In one of my previous books, *Spirit Games,* I suggest a large variety of fun games to help our children get past negative moments and find that more balanced state of mind from which problems can more easily be solved.

Playing games to learn cognitive and kinesthetic skills works for the same reasons. When we are in a positive frame of mind, we are present to that moment. It is in that state of acceptance that we are most open to new experiences and new knowledge.

We parents are our children's first teachers. We want them to be smart, we want them to enjoy themselves, we want to do what's good for them—and we want them to have fun with us.

Play *Smart Play* games and you can have it all.

EXPLANATION OF AGE CATEGORIES

Sometimes it is difficult to say at what age a child will do best with which game. There are some children who are delayed in their physical coordination but have exceptional control in their ability to use their hands and/or minds. Others don't want to sit and focus but have incredible large muscle coordination. Each child is unique.

The best way to know which games work best for your child or children is to try them out. Their enthusiasm or lack of it will let you know. You might find, as I often do, that children who I think are "too big" to be interested in that little kids' game are enthusiastic players. I like that, because they can be good models for the younger ones. For the purposes of this book, I've provided some general guidelines to age level, but feel free to make your own decisions.

Ages 6 and Under are games that will mostly appeal to the preschool/kindergarten set. There will be some two-year-olds who will be able to play many of the games and some six-year-olds who will be ready to move on to bigger challenges.

Ages 6 and Up are games that have slightly more involved directions and require more physical skills and a larger understanding of concepts.

All Ages are games with enough variability in them that siblings, friends of differing ages and abilities, and adults can all play them together.

HOW TO CONTACT THE AUTHOR

I have done workshops around the world where participants (teachers, aides, parents, therapists, and children) learned by playing. They had first-hand experience in playing *Self-Esteem Games, Spirit Games, Smart Play* games, and other games that can all be played in the family setting or in the inclusive classroom. They also learned how to make their own games and educational toys out of local and recyclable materials.

If you are interested in my services as a consultant or a workshop leader, simply e-mail me at: momsense@asis.com.

PART ONE

Games That Enhance Visual-Spatial Skills

Visual-spatial skills include an understanding of the shapes, images, patterns, designs, colors, and textures we see with our external eyes as well as all of the images we are able to conjure inside our heads. Spatial awareness includes the orientation of one's body to other objects in space and those objects' relationships to each other. Children who are strong in these skills are good at puzzles, reading maps, and finding their way around new places. They tend to think in pictures and images. They have opinions about colors that go together and textures that are pleasing; they enjoy visualizing, imagining, and "seeing with the mind's eye."

The games included in this part start with the basics: What are the colors, shapes, and sizes in our world? This information is presented in many ways, such as matching colors, jumping to shapes, and finding the prize under a certain size can.

These beginning games also help children be aware of things in the space around them and of how objects in that space relate to each other. In some games this is done with the whole body, as in one in which children pretend they are cars driving around and not bumping into each other. In other games it's done with the mind by making maps and doing puzzles.

Finally these games help children practice the art of visualizing things they cannot see with their eyes, such as the stars and their internal organs!

My Very Own Color Book

This is a game designed for the scribbler. Even if a child is only at the scribbling stage of her artistic development, she can still make her own book! This game shows her how, and it's fun for you, too. Sitting and quietly scribbling together can be a lovely bonding moment in itself. Then later, when you have something to "read" together many times, the pleasure of that moment is multiplied.

MATERIALS

paper
crayons, markers, colored pencils, or other drawing tools
ribbons, string, or plastic bag ties

DIRECTIONS

Take one piece of white paper, the heavier the better, and together scribble all over the page, using only one color. Then scribble another page, with another color. You can use crayons, markers, colored pencils, watercolors, pastels, chalks, or whatever else appeals to you.

After you have made a page for each color, poke some holes in the edges of the papers and tie the pages together using ribbon or string or plastic bag ties.

Read the book together and talk about the colors: "This is our blue page. There is some light blue here. It reminds me of the sky on a sunny day. This dark blue looks like the same color as my jeans. What else is blue in this room? You're right. My toenail polish is blue."

WHAT IS BEING LEARNED

Children are learning the names of colors and the variations of each color. They are learning that they can make a book. They are learning that their coauthor loves them so much that she wants to make and read a book together.

Color Run

I learned this game from a Montessori teacher who uses it as part of outdoor fun time. She likes it because it works out the children's extra energy while making them aware of colors and the world around them at the same time. What pleases her most is seeing the differences in the objects the children choose. One child, who was enthralled with nature, ran to touch the budding leaf of a flower for the color green. Another child, who prefers social interaction, ran after the first child because he was wearing a green jacket.

DIRECTIONS

When you and the children are outside, call out a color and have everyone scatter and run to something that is that color. For example, yell out "Yellow" and see who goes where to find what. Join in the fun and run, too. Consider it your workout for the day and a good excuse to avoid the treadmill at the gym.

Repeat the same color many times, as in "What else is yellow?" and let the children run and explore until they find, for example, that small buttercup hidden in the grass.

VARIATIONS

◆ Take a "Purple Walk." As you walk down the street, look for anything that is purple. Next time, choose a different color to look for.

- If no one is in the mood to move, play the color game of I Spy. One player says, "I spy the color ____," naming the color of something he sees outside or in the room. Then all the players try to guess which object was spied. When the object is identified, another player takes a turn at spying a color.

- For very little ones who don't know their colors yet, show an example of the color first. "See the blue color in your shirt? Find something else that is like that blue color."

WHAT IS BEING LEARNED

This is a color-learning game, of course, but it also helps to increase children's awareness of what's around them—their own everyday environment.

Distinguishing red from blue or brown from green is also another lesson in awareness—specifically, the differences and similarities between things. Whether it is seeing the difference between red and blue or noticing the similarities between blue and turquoise, children are sharpening their conscious awareness.

Color Dots

Two or more
people

Here's a fun way to teach colors because kids get to jump to them while they're learning. I find that children are always glad for an excuse to get out of their chairs, and teachers and parents are happy that the children are learning something while they are jumping around.

MATERIALS

colored construction paper
Optional: cardboard, tag board, nonslip material, glue

DIRECTIONS

To play this game, you need to make some color dots. The easiest way is to cut circles at least 6 inches in diameter out of different-colored construction paper.

If you want to get a little fancier and have the dots last for more than one game, glue the dots to cardboard or tag-board circles.

If you want the dots to last even longer, and not slip around when they are jumped on, buy some nonslip material, usually found at hardware stores or in the kitchen supplies section of a grocery store. Cut out circles that match the size of your dots and stick them to the bottom of the dots. Sandpaper works, too, if you are playing on a rug (but not on wooden floors, which could get scratched).

Not in the mood to cut out dots? The same game can be played just using pieces of colored paper.

Make at least six dots of different colors. Lay them randomly on the floor.

First, ask your player to jump from dot to dot.

Next, ask your player to jump to the color you call out. The jump from the red dot to the blue dot might be easy, but the jump from the red to the green might be a real doozy. Or, you can let the other players take turns calling out the colors the jumper should try to jump to.

VARIATIONS

♦ Chair to Dot: A player stands on a chair with the stack of color dots in her hand. She tosses them onto the floor and then calls out the color dot she wants to jump to.

♦ Dot to Dot: For this one, you'll need to make a few more sets of dots so that there are several of each color. Lay the color dots randomly on the floor and have the players jump to all the ones that are the same color. Some jumps may be easy if dots of the same color are close together. Others may be very far apart and more challenging, so the players have to jump "with all their might" to do it. Make sure kids know that making it to the dot isn't the important part—trying is.

You can also vary the way each player goes from dot to dot. Use a variety of directions, such as:

◇ Jump to all the red dots.

◇ Jump sideways to all the orange dots.

◇ Leap to all the blue dots.

◇ Jump backward to all the purple dots.

◇ Hop to all the greens dots.

◇ Jump and twirl to all the yellow dots.

◇ Jump to this sequence: red, then blue, then yellow, then green.

◇ Every time you land on a red dot, jump twice on the dot, and every time you land on a green dot, jump three times.

♦ Beanbag to Dot: Lay the dots down on the floor. Put down a marker to indicate where the player should stand. Give your player a beanbag. When you call out a color, the player throws a beanbag onto that color.

If your learner is very young, have a duplicate set of colors in your hand and say, "Throw the beanbag to the color that is the same as this."

WHAT IS BEING LEARNED

This game is about learning the colors, of course, but because it involves precise movements it also encourages an understanding of how much energy is needed to jump longer or shorter distances. Also, because it involves jumping, it enhances physical strength.

If your child does the variation of jumping from a chair, he is also learning to improve his sense of balance.

A child who does the variation of throwing a beanbag at the color is learning to improve eye-hand coordination, as well.

Match Me Up

One or two people

I once suggested this simple color-matching game and its variations to my teacher friend Lara. She had recently had a baby and was having difficulty with her three-year-old daughter, Lia. At first, Lia was charmed with her baby brother but then not so charmed when so much of her mother's attention was taken up by the new one. Lia started to get cranky and stubbornly defiant.

One morning they sat down and made this game and played it together. It took less than an hour and yet the mom reported that Lia was cheery all day. This game and its variations became one of those things that they could do together—and little brother couldn't! There's something about sitting down with your sweetie, being totally in the moment with her, and taking the time to play that tells her how much she matters to you.

You and your child can play this game alone or you can invite others to join in. Sometimes visiting relatives, for example, want to relate to your child but don't know how to initiate play. This game and its variations help elicit those bonding experiences.

The fun is multiplied if you and your child make the materials needed together or if older siblings make the games for younger ones.

MATERIALS

paper or index cards
felt-tip markers or crayons
Optional: colored construction paper, scissors

DIRECTIONS

Using small pieces of paper or index cards, make color-matching sets of red, blue, green, yellow, black, and white. Ask your child to help you make the cards using felt-tip markers or crayons. Let your child scribble away until the card is full.

You could also cut out squares of colored construction paper.

Then get ready to "play school." You pretend that you are the teacher and your child is the student. At first, place only two colors, such as red and blue, on the table. Give your player one of the matching cards and say, "Put the blue card on the other blue card" or "Put blue on blue." Next turn, add other choices so the player has to find the matching color out of three colors. Keep adding choices until all the colors are presented together and the player has to find the matching color out of six or more choices.

Remember to take turns. Sometimes she's the teacher and hands you the cards. If she's new to the game, you being the student each time will model for her how to match colors. It's important not to make this a testing situation. If your new learner gets it "wrong," simply state the facts.

"Okay, you put red on green. Let's look together and find the other red. Is it this one? No. That's yellow. What do you think about this one?"

VARIATIONS

There really is almost no limit to the variety of things that can be matched in this type of game for young children.

♦ Match identical flaps of cereal or cracker boxes.

♦ Match silhouette outlines of common objects, such as combs, spoons, and pencils, with the actual objects.

♦ Match shapes instead of colors. Cut out matching shapes, such as circles, squares, triangles, rectangles, and crosses, of the same color.

♦ Match textures using objects such as two cotton balls, two pieces of wax paper, two pieces of sandpaper, two macaroni noodles, two pieces of cellophane, two rubber bands, two pieces of sponge, two scraps of fabric, two pennies, two straws, and so on.

♦ Match written words. Start with family names and then add words of common objects or actions.

♦ You can even match smells by making your own scratch-and-sniff cards: Mix a scent, such as powdered cinnamon or cloves, perfume, or essential oils, with a texture, such as sand, salt, or glitter. Paint some glue on a card, pour on the scented texture, and let it dry. Shake off the excess and then have the players rub or scratch each of the cards and find the card with the matching scent.

WHAT IS BEING LEARNED

Knowing how things are the same and how they are different is the foundation for discrimination that helps us notice the details in life. We may start by noticing differences between colors or how the letter B is different from the letter P. Then, throughout our lives, we continue to notice more detailed differences: how to tell a crow from a raven; a Queen Anne chair from a Louis IV. Playing matching games with your child encourages a lifelong and rewarding awareness.

Everyone Wins Bingo

*Regular bingo can be hard for young ones when the tension builds as they
hope their bingo card fills up first and then someone else yells "Bingo!" I
know, that's life; some days you win and some days someone else wins.
But wouldn't it be nice if everyone could win? In this version of bingo for
the little ones, everyone does.*

MATERIALS

cardboard
pens
buttons or other markers

DIRECTIONS

Using the cardboard, make
bingo cards by writing numbers 1 to 10 or 10 to 20 on each
card. All the cards should have
the same numbers on them, but
in a different order. Give each
player a card and a pile of markers, such as buttons, cut-up pieces
of paper, coins, shells, or nuts in
their shells.

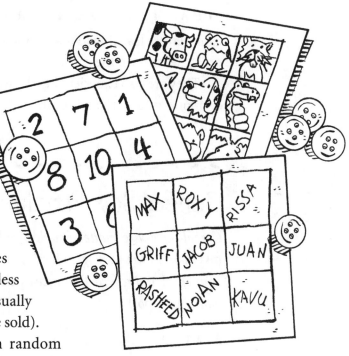

If you photocopied the cards, you
can use the bingo marker paint bottles
that "real" bingo players use (an odorless
version of this sponge-top bottle is usually
available wherever children's paints are sold).

As you call out each number in random
order, have the players find that number on their
cards and cover it with a marker.

When all of the numbers have been covered, go around to each player and say, "Got the 1 covered? Yep. Got the 2? Yep. Let's see if you got the 3. Oh, you did," and so on. When you've checked all the numbers, say, "It's a Bingo card! He has got Bingo, too!"

Believe me, the kids don't mind at all if everyone wins!

VARIATIONS

You can use this game to teach many things to young minds.

Make bingo cards using colors or shapes or letters or short words or people's names or animal pictures or whatever lesson you want to reinforce.

Instead of using buttons or other things as markers, you can make markers out of pictures or words on paper that players match to the pictures or words on the cards.

WHAT IS BEING LEARNED

Children are learning to match and recognize numbers or colors or shapes or whatever is on the card.

They are also experiencing the warm feeling that comes when they and everyone around them is doing well.

Cereal Box Puzzles

One or two people

Cereal boxes are made of such nice heavy cardboard, it seems a shame to toss them in the garbage. Here's a way you can make an instant puzzle for your child and recycle that nice cardboard at the same time. (Cracker boxes work well, too.)

MATERIALS

cereal box
scissors

DIRECTIONS

Cut out the front and back sides of the cereal box. Cut each side into two or more pieces depending upon the skill level of your child. For very little ones, cut the front side in half and show how the two parts can be put together to make a whole picture again. Then let him try completing the puzzle on his own. Cut the back side in half as well but use a diagonal cut this time so that you have two triangular halves.

Let your child play with these pieces until he gets the idea and can easily put the pieces together to make a whole picture. Then give him all four pieces and let him put the correct halves together.

For older children, cut the halves in half again so that there are now four pieces to each puzzle.

When your child is ready for an added challenge, cut the pieces in abstract shapes rather than just squares, triangles, or rectangles. If your child needs help with this type of puzzle, you can lay the puzzle on a piece of paper and outline each piece so he can see the shapes more clearly.

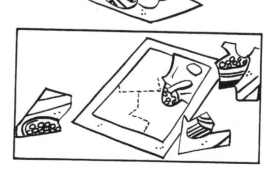

If you want to reuse the puzzles, they keep nicely in a brown mailing envelope. If you have another cereal box with the same design, cut that out and paste it on the envelope so your child can see which puzzle is inside.

VARIATIONS

◆ You can make the fastest puzzle ever (think: stuck in a waiting room with cranky kid) by tearing up a piece of paper.

◆ You can also make a more attractive (and less commercial-looking) puzzle by pasting a picture from a magazine on a piece of cardboard instead. Pictures from *National Geographic* or *Smithsonian* magazines work well.

WHAT IS BEING LEARNED

When they are doing puzzles, children must be very aware of shapes and how they match the empty spaces where pieces are needed. Puzzles also encourage children to notice similarities, such as how the color red or the bold line in one piece matches up to the same feature in another piece.

Match the Lids

One or two
people

A child's awareness of how some things are bigger than, smaller than, or the same size as other things comes at first with trial and error.

When you see young children trying to nest a series of cups, such as measuring cups where each cup is slightly larger than the next, you will notice that they don't immediately know that some cups are larger and will not fit into the smaller ones no matter how much force they apply. When force doesn't work, they experiment and find that small fits into big better than big fits into small!

Sometimes just saying the words "Try another way" can get them past the frustration of the cups not fitting and on to finding the way that they do.

MATERIALS

clean jars of different sizes and their lids

DIRECTIONS

Place a wide variety of jars with lids in front of your learner. Take all the lids off and toss them together, mixing them up.

Then give your child the challenge of finding the right lid for each jar.

With very young learners, you might want to start with just two jars and lids.

WHAT IS BEING LEARNED

Match the Lids shows children in a very direct way which sizes go together. If they are wrong, it doesn't fit!

Carny Game

One or two people

There is an old carnival gambling game—you probably know it—where an object is hidden under one of three cans and then the cans are quickly moved around to mix them up. You have to figure out under which can the object is hiding.

This is that same game, except that underneath the fun is the awareness of size, noticing that some things are bigger and smaller than others.

MATERIALS

three different-size cans, empty and cleaned and with labels removed
small object, such as fruit snacks

DIRECTIONS

Place the three different-size cans upside down on the table.

Put a small object under one of the cans. Foods such as fruit snacks are good objects to use because the child can eat it when he guesses the right answer. If your child is past the time of putting everything in his mouth, you might use something like a seashell or a marble that he gets to keep for each right answer.

Point out to your young player that the reward is being put under the big or medium or little can. Then mix up the cans and see if he can notice where the big can is and point to it. He's right? He gets the treat and/or praise and the chance to try again. Wrong? Look under the medium can together. "Nope, not there, in the medium-size can." Then the little one. "Nope, not under the small can." Now the big one. "Yeah. There it is! It was under the big can!"

VARIATIONS

Try hiding objects under containers of different shapes or colors. To get different-color cans, you could cover the same-size cans in different-color paper.

WHAT IS BEING LEARNED

Noticing the differences in sizes of objects is not automatic. It's information we pick up from experience. This is a fun way to get children to think about size discrimination.

It might take awhile for the little ones to see the difference in sizes or understand the concept of big, medium, and little. You might want to try using language that is more familiar to your child, such as the Papa-size can, the Mama-size can, and the baby-size can.

Full of Beans

One or two
people

This game is great for those times when the children are little and you really need time to get something done (like the dishes!). Just remember to put five bags of dried beans on your grocery list next time you go shopping. You can use them to keep the little ones occupied and learn lessons about size along the way.

MATERIALS

a large, clean plastic tub
5 bags of dried beans
unbreakable cups in different sizes
Optional: plastic water bottle

DIRECTIONS

Take a clean plastic tub, maybe an old baby bathtub or one that is used for washing dishes, and partially fill it with the dried beans. If you use a variety of beans, you'll get a more colorful mixture. If your child might be tempted to put small objects in her nose and ears, you'll want to either use larger beans, such as large lima beans, or sit with her while she is play-

ing and remind her as often as needed that "these beans are for pouring and playing. We don't put them in our noses. That can hurt us." (Children aren't being "bad" when they poke beans into different orifices, they are being little scientists exploring possibilities. It's our job to explain the downside of that kind of experimenting!)

Provide a variety of unbreakable cups in different sizes.

Holding the cups over the plastic tub, start your learners off by showing them how to pour beans from a small cup into a larger one and noticing how many times the small container is filled and emptied before the large container is full. Next show them that when they pour the beans from the big cup into the little one, the extra overflows.

Play a guessing game: Which holds more beans, the tall narrow cup or the short fat one?

You can provide a large funnel to add to the enjoyment. Or you can make a nice one by cutting a plastic water bottle in two. The bottom half is a cup and the top half is a funnel.

Let the children experiment on their own while you get those dishes done! Beans are also just fun to run your fingers through without any purpose at all.

VARIATIONS

♦ I know of one preschool that uses wild bird seed for this game and then sweeps outside whatever spills over for the birds to enjoy.

♦ You can also hide little treasures, such as refrigerator magnets or peanuts, in the beans for your child to find.

WHAT IS BEING LEARNED

This is a game that shows young ones in a very concrete and easily understandable way that things come in different sizes. They are learning about comparison—that some things are bigger than others.

If you're playing the variation about finding treasures in the beans, they are also developing their sense of touch.

Going to the Store

This game can be used to teach children about shapes, sizes, colors, and more, so children of different ages can play it together. It's also a game of something kids love to pretend to do: shop for food.

MATERIALS

food items

chairs, bench, or 2-by-4-foot board

table

DIRECTIONS

Go through the kitchen and gather up a bunch of food items—a box of cereal, a box of crackers, a can of soup, empty milk cartons, whatever. Put the food items on the table. The table is the "store."

Then make a "bridge" out of kitchen chairs lined up beside each other, a bench, or a 2-by-4-foot board on the floor.

You play the mother (how perfect is that!) and you ask each "shopper" to cross the "bridge" to go to the "store" and bring you back something. What that something is depends on the skill level of the child. Give younger children easier clues, such as something that is a specific color. Older children can get spelling or phonic clues.

If children are bringing back more than one item, give them a bag or a tray to carry the items in or on.

Suggestions for clues

♦ Something big or something small

♦ Something with yellow (or any other color) on the package

♦ Something with a square shape (or other shape)

♦ Something that starts with the sound *MMMM* (or any other phonic sound)

♦ Something that comes from cows

- ◆ Something that is made from flour
- ◆ Something that we eat for breakfast
- ◆ Two boxes and one can (or any other number combination)
- ◆ The item you are spelling, such as C-E-R-E-A-L

VARIATIONS

- ◆ Play this game in the real grocery store. Have your little one look for a box that has a certain color on it or is a certain shape. Use the same clues that you did at home if you want him to find the same food items.
- ◆ You can enlarge the learning taking place in the game by putting an older child at the "store" and have him take money and make change.

WHAT IS BEING LEARNED

Children are learning to recognize colors, shapes, numbers, and words in a play situation that models real life. Providing a wide variety of ways to learn the same thing makes the learning easier and makes it stick better.

If you make a "bridge" for the "shoppers" to cross and give them a tray to carry, they get an opportunity to practice their balancing skills. (Holding a tray means the children can't see their feet and have to rely on and increase their internal sense of balance.)

AGES 6 AND UP

Go Fish for Colors

Two or more people

Most young children like to play the traditional card game of Go Fish. But even older children can enjoy variations on this simple game. For example, when my kids were teens, we'd get through the tedious task of sorting socks by dealing out a "hand" of socks to each person, putting the rest in a paper bag, and playing Go Fish. ("Anyone have the mate to this green sock with the hearts on it?" "No, go fish in the bag.")

MATERIALS

colored paper or paint samples

DIRECTIONS

To play this version of Go Fish, make a set of "playing cards" by cutting pieces of colored paper into card shapes—two of each color. Try to find paper that is of more unusual colors than the basic red, yellow, green, and blue, such as turquoise, violet, or magenta. (Origami paper often comes in interesting shades.)

To make this game even more elaborate and to introduce a wide variety of shades to your player, get your "cards" at the paint or hardware store. The sample paint strips displayed there offer many different color variations. Choose very different colors for the younger set and more subtle variations for the older ones. Get two of each color you choose.

Deal out four or five cards to each player and put the rest, colored side down, on the floor or inside a paper bag.

The first player holds up one of her colors for all to see and says, "Does anyone have turquoise?" (or "this bluish color").

If no one has the matching color, the player has to Go Fish and picks a strip from the floor or out of the bag. (No peeking!) If it matches the one in her hand, she gets another turn. Otherwise, it's the next player's turn.

WHAT IS BEING LEARNED

Children are learning about new colors—beyond the basic red, blue, yellow, green, and purple.

Children can learn that there are many variations of blue, for example. One time when I was planning on painting the children's rooms, I asked them which colors they wanted. My five-year-old said, "Violet." I was so pleased she had a preference and knew that variation that I agreed, and together we painted her room violet.

Drive into the Empty Spaces

I was on a whirlwind workshop tour in New Zealand. I must have done twenty-three workshops in thirty days. We arrived in one town at midnight and the workshop was scheduled for early the following morning. I was happy, but exhausted. Then I got to the venue and found that instead of the usual group of thirty young teachers, there were ten prim teachers with gray hair and sensible shoes. I thought about canceling.

Then I heard an inner voice say "Let them play it out." At workshops I always introduce a wide variety of games, let the teachers play them for a few minutes to get the idea, and then go on to the next idea. "Playing it out" meant that I would instead introduce fewer games and let the teachers play them from start to finish. This would change the workshop from a repertoire of game activities to a workshop about playing.

"Playing it out" is what I did that day, and everyone was laughing and romping and playing so hard that we all sat panting and delighted at the end of the time. The workshop I had almost canceled turned out to be the most fun of them all.

Drive into the Empty Spaces is one of the games we played.

DIRECTIONS

Each player finds a partner. One of the partners is the "car" and the other is the "driver." The driver puts his hands on the car's waist and steers her around the room. With every driver moving at the same time, the challenge is to avoid collisions. The way to do that is to "Drive into the empty spaces." I purposely tell the drivers what to do instead of what not to do (as in "Don't bang into anyone else!") because children often don't hear the word "Don't." Instead, you've given them an idea that to some kids sounds like fun: "Bang into anyone else!"

Encourage the drivers to drive their cars as fast as they want, swerving

to find the empty spaces. Tell them or show them how they can add to the fun by making horn-honking or silly motor sounds.

Have the partners take turns being the car and being the driver.

If you have a large space, define it to make it smaller by using rope or chairs or instructions to limit where kids can drive ("stay on the rug"). The smaller the space, the more challenging the task of finding the empty spaces.

VARIATION

Put larger groups together to form two or more trains. The person at the head of the train is the "engineer." Engineers have to find the empty spaces through which to pull their trains. In this variation, the engineer has to be aware of how much space is needed to maneuver the whole train through that space so that even the "caboose" makes it through safely.

For sound effects, a "chug-a chug-a" noise replaces "vroom vroom" and train whistles replace honking horns.

WHAT IS BEING LEARNED

Young children don't yet have a complete awareness of the space around them. They'll often bang into one another. Any parent can tell you how often they get their toes stepped on by a child's foot or a nose banged by a child's flung arm. A child's sense of how big her body is and how much space it takes up is something that develops over time, especially considering that her body's size keeps changing!

In this game, an understanding of spatial relationships and an awareness of one's body are developed. Children need to be aware of where they are going and where the other person is going to avoid bumping into each other. This takes an awareness of space and of one's relationship to others in that space.

After the first game, you might ask the players which they liked better: being the car or being the driver. Did they prefer being the one in control or the one allowing someone else to make the decisions? Or were they equally satisfying? Both are useful traits, but it's always interesting to note their preferences.

Group
activity

Digestive Drama

Spatial relationships between things include both external and internal objects. Yet it's difficult to visualize these relationship between things we cannot see, such as the organs in the body or the celestial bodies in the sky. This game takes the concept out of the mental plane and into the physical plane where learners can kinesthetically experience these relationships.

Joe Crone, an elementary school teacher, has his students act out the digestive system process starting with the mouth, going through the stomach and intestines, and ending up out the end. His students choose the various body parts to act out. He even wrote a song about it that is part of his CD, Geometry Park, USA.

One day, he ran into a former student of his who said, "I remember your class well. I was the anus!"

DIRECTIONS

Have children take the roles of the different parts in the digestive process, including the role of the food.

You can chant these words to Joe's song or make up your own words.

> Digestion starts in the mouth
> Where the food's chewed up before it heads south.
> The salivary glands make it all wet
> And it's there that the food starts to digest.
>
> The esophagus squeezes the food on down
> And into the stomach, that's where it's found.
> The gastric juices break down the food
> And the stomach muscles churn it up so it can be used.
>
> The pancreas and liver add insulin and bile.
> It's in the duodenum for just a little while.
> The gooey, gooey muck is now called chyme;
> Its nutrients are taken in the small intestine.
>
> It's in the large intestine where the water's taken out.
> The chyme's compacted nicely, of this there is no doubt.
> It passes through the rectum, the anus is at the end.
> The sphincter muscles contract, your bowel movement begins.

[The chorus, which is optional, too:]

Chew it up and swallow those itty-bitty pieces

Take out all the good stuff. In the end it turns to feces.

Churn it up and swallow it, turn it into goo.

Now you get to sing those digestion blues.

VARIATIONS

♦ Other Physical Systems: Circulatory system: Act out the way blood takes fresh oxygen from the lungs and moves through the heart and arteries and returns through the veins.

♦ The Universe: Have children act out the solar system. One is the Sun and the others are the different planets revolving around the Sun while the Moon revolves around Earth.

Have children show the Sun and Earth and Moon pathways for one day. Where is the Sun at night? This is a good way to understand what happens in a solar eclipse, when the Moon comes between Earth and the Sun, and a lunar eclipse, when Earth comes between the Sun and the Moon.

♦ What Time Is It?: Players are clock faces and their arms are the clock hands. Where are their arms when it is three o'clock? six o'clock? twelve o'clock? twelve-thirty? ten minutes after three?

♦ Atom Arrangement: The players act out different molecular structures. How many protons, neutrons, and electrons are there in H_2O? How do they relate to each other? How does that relationship change when H_2O is combined with sulfur to form sulfuric acid?

WHAT IS BEING LEARNED

Students are learning how objects relate to one another in both internal and external space.

ALL AGES

Jump the Shapes

Two or more people

This is a no-fail game. I have played this game in so many countries with so many different kids that I can guarantee kids will jump for it. This game is also rich in variations. It can be easy; it can be challenging; and it can even help kids learn their shapes, numbers, letters, and colors.

One time this game saved me. I was giving my first workshop in Cambodia and I wanted it to go well. My interpreter, my daughters, and I were driven to the orphanage where I expected I would be giving a talk to the director and her staff on child development, the benefits of play, and how to make learning toys from throwaway materials. Instead of just a small group of adults, thirty excited children met our car. They were all there for the talk!

I knew there was no way these children were going to sit still while I espoused theory, so it was time for a fast change of plans. I wasn't going to tell them about the benefits of play or what children needed, I was going to show them—right now! My daughters got the kids coloring on newspaper while I quickly drew colorful shapes on six newspaper sections. Then, with the help of the interpreter, we soon had the kids taking turns jumping to each shape while the other children called out the shape's name in their language.

The children loved playing this game, so my daughters and I had enough time to look around the room and find things to make into more games (benches lined up to make a balance beam, newspaper scrunched up to make balls, bull's-eyes drawn on blackboards to make targets, and so on).

At home, you can make this game a bit mysterious the first time you play it. For example, one day when the kids are running around and you want them to focus their energy, do this: start setting up the game. Add to the mystery by not saying, if you're asked, what you are doing. Just murmur an enticing "You'll see."

By the time you are done, the children will be gathered round and ready for whatever!

MATERIALS

newspaper or typing paper or construction paper
markers or crayons
tape
Optional: scissors

DIRECTIONS

Pull out six to nine newspaper pages. Fold the pages in half and draw a shape on each with markers or crayon. Or, you can cut each page into a different shape. Start with the ordinary shapes—circle, square, rectangle, triangle, and star—and later, or if you have older children playing, add shapes such as pentagons, octagons, hexagons, and rhomboids.

Tape each newspaper page on the floor, one right above the other, forming a vertical line. (The more pages you use, the harder the game.)

Start off simply by jumping forward from one shape to the next, inviting the children to follow you. Call out the shapes as you land on them. Do it a few times, always starting from the first shape and jumping on each shape until the last one.

Then call out different shape names for each child to jump to. For younger children, keep the instructions short ("Jump from the square to the circle"). For older children, make the instructions longer ("Jump from the circle to the triangle to the octagon").

If you want to increase a child's ability to remember, or if you want to make the game more interesting for an older sibling or playmate, make the instructions increasingly complicated, such as "Walk on your heels to the

star, tiptoe to the rectangle, and hop four times on the circle." Or, "Jump sideways to the square and then backward to the triangle and then over the next three ones and land on the pentagon." Or, "Hop on your left foot to the square, then twirl in the air and land on the hexagon."

VARIATION

Instead of making shapes on the newspaper pages, draw different colors, numbers, or letters on each section.

WHAT IS BEING LEARNED

There is so much to learn from these games. Children learn about shapes (or colors or numbers or letters), plus they improve their balance by jumping and hopping. They are also learning to move their bodies in a variety of ways.

When you ask players to follow a series of instructions, you're also improving their memory skills—their ability to listen, remember, and do it.

But, most of all, playing Jump the Shapes gives you and the children the awareness of the rich variety of games that can be played with something as common as yesterday's news.

Obstacles Galore

On a rainy day, you can turn any room into a fun zone with this game. Set up the first course yourself, but once the kids get the idea of how to do it, let them come up with their own ideas. My agile children would come up with ways of moving through the obstacle course that I never would have thought of—and couldn't do if I wanted to! ("Let's see, your plan is that we jump down from the top of the dresser onto the bed, do a somersault from the bed onto the floor, and then wiggle under the bed to get to . . .")

MATERIALS

furniture
Optional: bell or tambourine, or drum, or some other noisemaker

DIRECTIONS

Use the furniture to make an obstacle course.

Think prepositions. You want something to go *under,* something to go *over,* something to go *around,* something to go *between,* and something to go *across.*

Think directionally: something to climb *up,* something to go *down,* something to go *into,* and something to go *out of.*

Think action verbs: something to *jump* over; something to *climb* on; something to *skip* around; something to *walk* forward, backward, or sideways to; something to *crawl* to or under; and something to *run* to.

Mark the start of the obstacle course with a piece of paper or rug or anything that defines that space as the beginning. This rule helps kids not cut in front of each other and gives some order to the game if many children are playing together. I like to add a bell or noisemaker of some kind at the end to signal a successful completion. I find children really like ringing a bell or shaking a tambourine to announce their triumph to the world. Children can go one after the other or they can take turns going through with everyone applauding each person's success.

Here are some suggestions for obstacles:

♦ A table to go under

♦ Two rows of chairs to go between

♦ A stool to skip around

♦ A stack of books to jump over

♦ A chair to stand on and jump down from

♦ A line in the linoleum pattern to walk backward on

♦ A box to sit in and wiggle forward

♦ A bench to walk across sideways

VARIATION

Play the game outside on a nice day, using obstacles like:

♦ A fallen log to cross over

♦ A tree to skip around

♦ A rock to climb up and jump off

♦ Sidewalk squares to jump on, from one to another

♦ A street lamp to run to, touch, and run back from

WHAT IS BEING LEARNED

A lot of different types of learning are taking place in this game that will help children and please their teachers and parents. First of all, children are learning about relating objects to one another by making a course. They are learning about their relationship to these objects—for example, that some things are lower than they are and that they have to adjust their body to wiggle under them. Teachers will be glad that children are also learning lessons about prepositions, directions, and action verbs in a way that is meaningful to them. Gym teachers will like seeing children enhancing their motor skills by using a variety of movements. And parents will be glad to see that their children can be inventive and find active ways to entertain themselves.

Internal Map

One or two people

I don't know about you, but I get lost easily. I don't mind asking for directions, but I wish I had learned at an earlier age how to develop an internal awareness of where I am in space.

One way to help children develop this awareness is to have them try to mentally project themselves upward in order to get a bird's-eye view of how things around them are related to each other.

A good way to start is with the things in the child's own house or classroom.

MATERIALS

piece of paper
Optional: blindfold or large paper bag

DIRECTIONS

Put a piece of paper on the floor for the child to stand on. Call this paper "home base." While your child stands on home base, ask him to notice how far it is to different objects in the room, such as the bookshelf, the couch, the kitchen door. Then have him notice the distance from the bookshelf to the couch, from the couch to the kitchen door, and from that door to home base.

Next, ask him to close his eyes and walk from home base to each of the objects named, in turn. For example, "Walk to the bookshelf and then back to home base without opening your eyes."

If he's heading off in the wrong direction or about to bump into something, give him some help by gently guiding him back on track.

Once he's made it to each of the first locations, you can make the instructions more complicated. For example, "Walk to the bookshelf and then from there to the couch and from there to the kitchen door and then back to home base."

Some children might have a hard time not opening their eyes to peek, so you might want to use a blindfold. (I've found that many kids prefer a large paper grocery bag on their head instead of a blindfold. It doesn't slip down or get tangled in their hair the way a blindfold might.) And, of course, you will want to clear the space of any potential shin busters, such as coffee tables, and things that might cause the child to trip, such as toys on the floor or slippery scatter rugs.

VARIATIONS

♦ Where Is It?: Scrunch up a piece of paper to form a ball, or use any small object, and place it a distance away from home base. Ask your player to close his eyes and then walk to where he thinks the paper is and pick it up. This is harder than it sounds. Try it yourself when it's your turn.

   To make the game more complicated, have the child pick up two or more objects from different locations. The player goes to the first location and from there to the next without opening his eyes.

♦ Where Am I?: Have children draw a map of the area surrounding where they live.

WHAT IS BEING LEARNED

Children are developing a sense of where things are in space relative to themselves and relative to each other.

Kangaroo Ball

Group activity

When children are jumping kangaroos who are either trying to bump or avoid getting bumped by other jumping kangaroos, they'll get plenty of experience in spatial relationships! This game helps children notice where they are in space, what's around them, and what's coming at them.

Kangaroo Ball is also a wonderful outlet for excess energy, so it's great for a birthday party when you want something that will burn off the sugar the children just ate. That's a benefit you just don't get from Pin the Tail on the Donkey.

MATERIALS

"gentle balls" (simple balls made out of newspaper or plastic bags scrunched up and taped closed, see page 125) or store-bought foam balls

DIRECTIONS

Each player starts with a ball on the floor in front of her. The players then squat down and, using their knees, pick up their balls. Then, holding the balls between their knees, they jump around like kangaroos. Call out different kinds of jumps for the players to do, such as:

- ♦ short jumps
- ♦ long jumps
- ♦ sideways jumps
- ♦ fast jumps
- ♦ slow jumps
- ♦ jumps over something, such as a piece of paper

Have the players count, if they want to, how many of each kind of jump they can do without dropping the ball.

VARIATION

In the regular game, children have to avoid bumping into each other so they don't lose their ball. In this variation, you tell them that they can bump hips (gently) to see if they can get other players to drop their balls while not losing their own ball. Many children will find this variation the most fun of all. But you know your players best. It could invite trouble if the players tend to be raucous.

WHAT IS BEING LEARNED

Besides developing their awareness of space so that they don't (or do) bump into others, children are developing their lower body strength by jumping and gripping the balls with their legs. When they try different ways of moving, they are developing their ability to isolate and use different muscle groups.

Two or more
people

Popsicle Stick Puzzle

If you have children, Popsicle sticks are probably pretty common in your life. It doesn't take but a second to wash the sticky stuff off the stick after the Popsicle is gone and put it on the windowsill to dry. Once you've collected four or five sticks, you can make this nifty puzzle. Collect more, or purchase craft sticks at a hobby shop, and two or more can play.

MATERIALS

Popsicle sticks, craft sticks, or tongue depressors
tape
felt-tip pens

DIRECTIONS

Lay four or five sticks next to each other as if making a raft. Then tape the sticks together on one side. Draw a picture using felt-tip pens, or make a simple bold design that covers all or most of the untaped side of the "raft."

Next, untape the sticks and give the pieces to your learner. Explain that he should put the pieces together to re-form the picture.

Put together another set of Popsicle sticks and have your learner draw his own puzzle for you to put together.

If there are many people making puzzles, pass the puzzles around so everyone gets a chance to try each one.

VARIATIONS

Instead of drawing your own picture, paste a picture from a magazine on the sticks. Then separate the sticks with a sharp knife or scissors.

Instead of using four or five sticks, use many more to make a much larger puzzle. The design can be as simple or as complicated as each designer wants, so this is an activity all ages can play.

WHAT IS BEING LEARNED

Children are learning that there are parts to a whole. Unlike a regular puzzle, which is about finding the right shape, this puzzle encourages a sense of combining the different elements of a larger picture. By noticing, for example, how a curved line on one piece matches the line on another, they are seeing the continuity of how things relate to each other in space.

Blind Portraits

Two or more people

In this game, children will draw each other's portraits. The trick is that they aren't allow to look at their paper while they are doing it.

The results are often amusing and sometimes impressive. Maybe this is how Picasso got his inspiration!

MATERIALS

colored or regular pencils

paper

DIRECTIONS

Give your players pencils and paper and have two players, such as you and your child, sit facing each other. Then the two players draw each other without ever looking down at the paper until they are finished drawing.

VARIATION

Draw something in the room without looking at the paper.

WHAT IS BEING LEARNED

This activity encourages the artists to keep an internal awareness of where their hand is on the paper in reference to the features or objects they are drawing.

The activity also encourages children to concentrate, focus their attention, and notice details—skills very much needed in school and in life!

Connect to a Star

Two or more
people

Learning activities that use movement are fun, but there is a lot to be learned from just being still. In this visualization game, stillness, imagination, and a belief in one's inner wisdom rule.

Connecting to a star, if done in the evening, can help children integrate the day's experiences. In the morning, it's a way to focus and fill their bodies with energy for the day ahead.

DIRECTIONS

Ask the players to sit cross-legged with their spines straight and hands relaxed. Give these instructions: "First, let's take four deep breaths. Take a big breath in through your nose and imagine that you are filling your belly up with air; let your stomach expand, then let that air fill up your lungs and let your chest expand. (pause) Now empty the air out of your mouth and then out of your chest, letting your chest deflate; push the last of the air out of your belly by pulling in on your stomach muscles."

After the four deep breaths, return to normal breathing pattern and add the following:

"Imagine that there is a shining star right above your head, the kind that radiates starshine from each of its points. One of those points is pouring energy to the top of your head. Take a breath and imagine that energy is coming down through the crown of your head and down your spine, and exhale it right out the base of your spine into the ground under you.

"This energy keeps going down into the earth, all the way down, until it reaches the center of the planet. Then inhale, and all this deep earth energy travels back up the same way and enters the base of your spine. It travels up until it goes back out the top of your head and right up to the star, making the star shine even brighter.

"Then exhale all that bright white energy that comes down from the star right into your head again. It travels down your spine and leaves your body to go back to the center of the earth."

"Now inhale that earth energy up again, through your spine, and this time breathe out and let it spill out through the top of your head like a waterfall, showering and enveloping your body.

"Do this three more times, going at your own pace, starting with the star above your head and ending with a waterfall of star glitter."

At the quiet end of this session, suggest to the players that this is a good time to pose a question to themselves, such as: "What should I do about this problem I'm having?" Suggest that they can expect the answer to come—if not right away, then later in some form, such as an overheard remark, a phrase in a book or song, a friend's advice that feels very right . . .

WHAT IS BEING LEARNED

Children get practice in visualizing and seeing with their mind's eye. Also, learning to be still and access the quiet intelligence within is a skill we all need all our lives. This game gives children one way to develop that ability.

Two or more
people

Label Art

If you're like me and you enjoy wandering around large office supply stores, you probably know that they have a lot of things that can entertain children. For one daughter's fifth birthday, I bought a file box from an office supply store and filled it with interesting office things: stapler and staples, a variety of pens, index cards, colored tapes, glue sticks, and self-stick labels in a variety of shapes, among other things. You would have thought I had brought her the moon. She and her sister had great fun playing games such as Office with all the stuff. But it was the self-stick labels that really brought out the artists in them.

MATERIALS

self-stick labels, such as mailing labels, file labels, colored dots, and
Post-its
paper or index cards

DIRECTIONS

Buy a variety of labels and let your child make designs or figures out of them by sticking them on a piece of paper or card. For example, he can make a simple stick figure with a round label for a head, rectangles for the arms, and a square for the body. He could make one animal figure or a whole zoo of animals.

There's also no end of abstract designs that can be made.

Suggest to your artist that he use his art to make his own greeting cards, such as for Daddy's birthday.

WHAT IS BEING LEARNED

This is all about creativity. When there is no right or wrong way to do something, imagination is free to do whatever it wants. Because it is easy to do, young children can play and stick right alongside an older sibling and all can feel a sense of accomplishment.

PART TWO

Games That Enhance Verbal-Language Skills

These skills involve the knowledge of language, including reading, writing, and speaking. They involve knowing the meaning of words and understanding idioms and plays on words. Children who are strong in these skills are good at playing word games, making up stories, debating, creative writing, and telling jokes. They have good reading comprehension and tend to think in words.

To give children the start they need in verbal-language skills, this section offers pre-reading games, which involve the recognition of letters by sight, by touch, and with the whole body. There are beginner's reading games that start with an autobiographical book, as well as an advanced reader's dictionary game.

Because developing language skills requires an ability to listen well, there are also games in which hearing is very much a part of the playing.

AGES 6 AND UNDER

- -

Book in a Baggie

One or two
people

This is the best idea I've heard of for a quick, fun, and easy book for your little ones that is all about them. I don't know who first thought of putting photos in sandwich bags, but it's one of those great ideas that needs to be passed on.

It's also a good way to use those photos that weren't good enough to make the family photo album but are too precious to throw away. If your photos are still in the shoe box and unlikely to ever make it to an album, here's a good motivator to put them somewhere where they will be seen and will become your child's keepsake.

MATERIALS

photos
plastic sandwich bags
stapler
Optional: paper

DIRECTIONS

Have your child help you select family photos that he would like to include in the book. Encourage him to pick a photo for each member of the family, including grandparents and pets. Put a photo, or two photos back to back, in each sandwich bag.

Once you have filled four or five bags, staple the open sides together to form the pages of the book. You might even want to staple a cover on the book and title it using your child's name, such as "Jacob's Family and Friends" or "People Jacob Loves" or "People Who Love Jacob." You can be sure this will be a book your child will want to see again and again. After all, he is the star!

Include captions to each photo or make a story to go with the pictures in the book so that you have something to read when you look at the book. You can write the captions on pieces of paper and slip them inside the plastic bags or paste them on the outside. Write a sentence or two, such as "Here is Jacob petting doggie Daisy. He loves his dog." Or write it from the child's perspective: "Here I am petting my doggie. I love him." You can make up what to write yourself or let your child decide what the sentence will say. When I let my youngest do that, she wanted me to write under one photo of me looking at her, "This is my mom loving me."

Instead of sentences, you could also write just one word, such as "Grannie," so that your new learner will begin to recognize words and can "read" the book to you. In this case, instead of putting the word on a piece of paper inside the bag or underneath the photo, paste it like a flap over the photo. The child then learns to read the word and lift the flap to see if he was right. (It *is* Grannie!)

VARIATIONS

For a more elaborate book, take and include photos of your home, your child's bedroom, the local playground, or any other place where your child spends a lot of time.

You could also plan to take pictures that depict events in your child's day from morning to night for a book entitled "Jacob's Life" or "People and Places in Jacob's Day." For example, the first shot could show Jacob waking up, the next having breakfast, followed by going to the sitter's, playing with friends, getting picked up by Mommy, eating dinner with the family, and so on, until it ends with snuggling and reading that good-night story.

If you want your photo book to be more substantial than plastic bags, it's possible to purchase just the pages that go into photo albums without buying the album. I like the kind that has an adhesive quality to the covering plastic so the photos stay secured to the page. Buy a bunch of these and tie them together with a ribbon.

What Is Being Learned

There is so much for your child to learn from having his own book. The most important being that he is very important! A whole book that is all about him means that he matters very much and that the person who made it must think so, too.

If you do a book about the sequences in your child's day, it can reduce the possibility of anxiousness when in a new situation, such as being left at preschool or with a baby sitter. Because he's read the book, he knows how it ends: his loved one comes and gets him and takes him home.

When you add words, whether it's a sentence for the older child or a single word for the little one, you are helping your child learn to read.

Name Matches

Children learn they have a name of their own when they are quite young. A little later they discover that their name can be written and read. This game aids that discovery.

One or two
people

Materials

pen
paper
scissors
Optional: glue stick

Directions

Write your child's name on a sheet of paper in large block letters.

Write it again on the bottom of the sheet and cut this version out, separating each letter into its own square.

With your child on your lap or next to you, pick up the first letter of her name and help her find the matching letter on the sheet of paper.

If you want, you can have her glue the letter on top of the matching letter with a glue stick. If she is too young to maneuver a glue stick, a little lick on the back of the paper will make it stick well enough for this game.

VARIATIONS

Add other letter choices so she has to distinguish the letters in her name from all other letters.

Do the same game with the names of other family members.

WHAT IS BEING LEARNED

Children are learning that their name can be made out of letters, as well as learning individual letter names.

Learn to Read in Five Minutes or Less!

One or two people

When working with children in their homes, I have fun bragging to the parents that I can teach their child to read in five minutes, especially if I can tell that the parents are doubtful about their child's ability to learn to read. This is how I do it.

MATERIALS

    index cards
    pencil

DIRECTIONS

On separate index cards, write down the names of the child's family or other meaningful people (or animals) in his life, such as Mommy, Daddy, Susie (the sister), Jim (the uncle), and Rex (the dog).

Start with two cards and announce to everyone, including the child, that he will be able to read these words.

In private, talk to the child about ways to recognize each name. For example, Mommy's name starts with a letter that looks like a mountain. Daddy's name has a half circle in the front. Grandly mix up the two cards as if you're shuffling well and have him practice recognizing the symbols. If his attention has been engaged and excited by the game, don't be surprised if he easily knows the word the first time. If he doesn't, and still enjoys the game, talk a little more about the differences in the words—for example, "Mommy" is long and "Dad" is short. Don't hesitate to supply the correct answer if needed. This is a game, not a test!

When the child is ready, invite in his audience and let him shine. Remember to shuffle with a flourish so no one can claim that the child just memorized the order of the names! When he is ready, add the other names. Point out that Susie's name starts with a letter that looks like a snake and Jim's first letter looks like an upside-down candy cane. Have the child practice recognizing the different names; it won't take long before he is ready for his next performance.

Show the first card with the mountain letter and watch him say proudly "Mommy." The upside-down candy cane letter makes the child proclaim "Jim," and so on.

VARIATIONS

Make index cards for various objects in the house and tape them onto those objects. Start with just a few words. For example, tape the card "door" onto the door, the word "desk" on the desk, "refrigerator" on the fridge, and so on. Leave the cards taped up and let your child just absorb the words.

One day, make a duplicate set of cards. The game is for your child to find the matching cards. For example, give him an index card that says "door" and let him look around the room and find the matching word. ("You found the word that says 'door'—you are such a brilliant boy!")

WHAT IS BEING LEARNED

Children learn that those silly scribbles on a printed page actually stand for words and that words can be read and understood.

They learn to start paying attention to the details of the shape of each letter, noting that each letter has its own shape and sound.

They also learn that it is possible for *them* to begin to make sense of those scribbles, and that is truly an enormously satisfying experience.

Alphabet Fishing

One or two
people

If you have young children, you probably already have a set of those magnetized letters that stick to the refrigerator. The kids probably played with them at first and in a productive moment might even have arranged them, with your help, into the order of A to Z. Maybe one day you might have made a message out of them. Usually a few get lost and mostly they are just forgotten things on the fridge.

Here's a way to use those letters to make a game that I play with preschool children. It's a fun way to learn recognition of letters (and numbers if you have both).

MATERIALS

> small magnet
> string
> pencil
> magnetized letters or sturdy paper and paper clips

DIRECTIONS

Take a magnet and tie (or tape) a piece of string around it. Tie the other end of the string to a pencil. That is your fishing pole.

Lay the letters down on the floor so that the small internal magnet is facing up. Spread them out so they aren't touching each other.

If you don't have magnetized letters, cut some fish shapes out of index cards or other durable paper. Write a letter on each fish and spread them out on the floor or in a box. It's helpful to include the letters that are often reversed by new writers, such as B, D, P, Q, G, and S. Attach a paper clip to each fish.

Have your child stand over the letters dangling his fishing pole and see which letters he catches.

It helps to show excitement over each letter he catches. Lay them out faceup so he can proudly display his catches.

This is not a test. It isn't necessary to say "And what letter is this?" It's more important to get enthusiastic about each letter. "Let's see what you caught! You got an . . . N!" You could pause slightly before you say the letter to give your child a chance to show off the letters he does know.

If you have several players, you can make poles for all of them and have them fish at the same time. The older players can put their letters together to form words.

VARIATIONS

♦ Sort and Count: Some alphabet sets have more than one of each letter. This gives you the perfect opportunity to introduce the concepts of sameness and of counting. "Let's see, you caught an A. Now, didn't you catch a letter that was the same as this one? Where is that one? Oh, you're right—here it is. Look, now you have three A's. Let's count them together—one, two, three."

♦ What Letter Is Missing?: Place a few of the letters in front of the player and ask him to look away or cover his eyes as you remove one letter from the group. When the player uncovers his eyes and looks at the letters, ask if he knows which one is missing.

WHAT IS BEING LEARNED

This game will help make letters and numbers increasingly familiar and friendly to your learner. You can expand on the game by making connections for him between the game letters and daily life. "Remember that letter S you caught yesterday when you were fishing? There it is again in that stop sign. Look, there are two more of those S's in that sign that says 'crosswalk' and another in that sign that says 'store'. Gosh, there are S's all over the place!"

Polka-Dot Letters

Two or more people

Learning to write letters is a way for children to thrill the adults in their lives, but it can only go so far as a motivator. However, if they write a letter again and again and suddenly produce a magic result, as in this game, that's an exciting new reason to do it.

MATERIALS

crayons
paper
paper clip

DIRECTIONS

Have your little one go over and over the same large letter with many different crayon colors, making sure the last color that is used is black. Or you can take turns, each applying the next coat of color.

Then have the child scratch little circles in the black color with the end of a paper clip or toothpick and watch as the other colors come through. You end up with a polka-dot letter!

VARIATION

Scratch stripes or crisscrosses or any other kind of shape instead of polka dots.

WHAT IS BEING LEARNED

This is a good way to reinforce how letters are formed. As you describe the process to your child, you also enlarge his language vocabulary by using prepositions (down, up, around, and so on).

For example, you might say, "Let's make a polka-dot D, Dylan. It's the first letter of your name. We'll start at the top and go down. Then we'll start at the top and go around. Here, let's both hold the crayon and we'll do it together. The top and down; the top and around. The top and down; the top and around. Now, let's color in the whole letter. Good! Which color should we use next?"

Sand Letters

Kindergarten teachers get to make these letters all the time. Why should they have all the fun? Playing this game is a lovely way to spend some time with your children and help them learn the alphabet with art that teaches!

Two or more people

MATERIALS

glue
index cards or heavy paper
Optional: paintbrush
sand, salt, or rice
Optional: paint

DIRECTIONS

Use a glue bottle to squeeze a letter's shape onto an index card or piece of heavy paper. Or paint the glue letter on the paper with a brush.

Have your child cover the wet glue with generous amounts of sand, salt, or rice.

Let the glue dry. When it does, shake off the excess sand, salt, or rice.

If you want to get fancy, you can mix a little paint into separate piles of the sand, salt, or rice and use this to make rainbow letters. You can also buy colored sand.

Make a whole set of sand letter and use them to help your child learn the alphabet by feeling the letters' shapes.

VARIATIONS

Here are some games to play with sand letters:

♦ Ask the player to put her hands behind her back. Then slip one of the letters into her hands. Can she guess what the letter is by feeling it?

♦ Place several letters on the table. Put a blindfold on the player and ask her to find the letter you request by feeling for it.

♦ Ask an older player to make a word out of some letters laid out on the table while the blindfolded player has to find the letters by feel.

♦ See if the player can identify a letter using only her bare feet, or her cheeks, or her elbow!

WHAT IS BEING LEARNED

Sand letters are such good tools to teach the alphabet because learners use the sense of touch as well as sight. Whenever more than one sensory pathway is being used, deeper learning is taking place.

Alphabet Instant Letters

This game is such a simple and fun way to learn or play with the alphabet that I wonder why it's not available commercially. Maybe it is, but it's so easy to make that no one buys it. The idea came to me in a dream, and it is a dream game because you can play it with your child while waiting at the doctor's office, sitting in an airplane, or anywhere you are stuck for a while and need to entertain yourselves. All you need is a piece of paper.

MATERIALS

piece of paper

DIRECTIONS

Take a piece of paper and tear or cut out some thin rectangles and a few circles. Tear the circles in half and tear the rectangles in various lengths. If you want to, tear the center out of the half circles so they form the letter C.

If you want to replay the game later, make the pieces last longer by using heavier paper, such as colored construction paper, index cards, poster board, or magazine covers.

Using these pieces of paper, make the different letters of the alphabet.

It's a delightful surprise that you can make every letter with just these simple shapes.

If your child is new at learning letters, you could make the first one for her to copy.

She could make a letter while you look the other way and then you look at it and name it. Take turns.

If your child is young and just wants to play with the shapes, let her make whatever configuration she wants and name the ones that accidentally turn out to be letters or shapes. "You just made the letter L!"

Make little words like "cat" and "hat" or "pen" and "hen" or "mad" and "sad," where you can change the word just by replacing the first letter. (I'd hesitate to make a two- or three-word sentence because a breeze or a stray hand might mess up the letters and replace fun with frustration.)

WHAT IS BEING LEARNED

When you saw the Greek alphabet or Japanese characters for the first time, it might have seemed amazing to you that people could read those symbols. Children feel the same way when they see words.

It's nice to know that those mysterious things called letters that make up words are nothing more than lines and half circles. Once your learner can make them and know them, she's well on her way to becoming a reader.

If your child is at the stage in his writing when some letters are being written backward, here is a nonjudgmental and active way to help him be aware of the different directions. For example, you could make a letter b and pretend the letter is moving forward: "Zoom—here goes the letter b. Zoom. Zoom. Uh-oh, the b is turning around and going backward! Will you turn b around so it can go forward again. Silly b. It's going the wrong way."

Letter Hopscotch

Two or more
people

Hopscotch is a game that many children play, and once they are familiar with how to do the game, you can enlarge what they learn incidentally by using letters instead of numbers.

MATERIALS

masking tape or stick or chalk
stone or beanbag

DIRECTIONS

Make the hopscotch diagram (see illustration). You can make it on the floor using masking tape, outside on asphalt or cement using chalk, or in the dirt using a stick. If you are using chalk or dirt, it is easier to change the letters and play again.

Instead of using the usual numbers inside the diagram, mark letters in the spaces.

Have each player in turn throw a marker, such as a stone or beanbag, to the letter you or another player names. The player then has to jump or hop to all the other letters, leading up to the one with the marker on it, pick up the marker, and jump to the end and then back to the starting point.

VARIATIONS

You can use the regular hopscotch movements, if you know them, or you can change the pattern of the jumping and hopping to suit each player's abilities or interests. Some possibilities are:

♦ Broad jumping from the starting point to the letter named

♦ Going in a sequential patterns, that is, jumping on each letter in the order it occurs in the alphabet

♦ Jumping only on the uppercase letters or only on lowercase letters

WHAT IS BEING LEARNED

Children learn to begin to recognize letters and to distinguish upper- from lowercase. They also get practice in balance when they hop and in motor planning when they jump from square to square.

Musical Movements

In this listening game, each sound calls for a different movement. Add enough different sounds and you've got a memory game, as well!

MATERIALS

different musical instruments

DIRECTIONS

Using musical instruments, assign a movement to each sound. For example, ask the children to twirl when they hear the bell, jump when they hear the tambourine, hop when they hear the flute, bounce when they hear the drum, and so on.

First play each instrument so that the children can rehearse the movements. Then turn your back so they can't see which instrument you are going to play. Play each instrument one at a time for random periods of time so they really have to listen and change their movements when you change instruments. Then try playing two instruments at once so they are, for example, hopping while twirling.

VARIATION

Have the children take turns playing the instruments. Place the music makers in a line facing you, their backs to the dancers. You be the orchestra leader and point your baton at the child whose instrument you want played. Or the orchestra faces the dancers and you tap the back of the person who is holding the instrument you want played.

WHAT IS BEING LEARNED

Listening and memory are enhanced with this game. A person's ability to speak is directly related to the ability to listen and remember.

AGES 6 AND UP

Sounds True

If you haven't yet gone digital in your photographing, you might have some leftover empty film canisters. Even if you don't, they are easy enough to find at places that develop film.

Using these canisters, you can easily make a game that sharpens your child's listening skills.

MATERIALS

small items found around the house
about 10 empty film canisters

DIRECTIONS

Put an equal amount of each of the small item you chose inside two canisters. For example, put salt in two of them, rice in another two, popcorn in another two, and so on. Other good choices include buttons, gravel, beans, sand, and pennies.

Give one canister of each kind to your player and keep one of each kind yourself.

Shake one of your cans and ask your player to find the canister that makes the same noise.

Next, it's her turn to shake a can and your turn to find the matching one from your set.

Some sounds may be easy to distinguish, such as the difference between the noise pennies make and the noise rice makes.

Telling the difference between the sounds of salt and sand requires more attentive listening.

VARIATION

Take turns making up a beat with your sounds for your learner to play with you. For example: Shake the salt canister twice, the bean canister four times in a simple 2:4 beat. Repeat the beat many times and encourage your youngster to make the same rhythm with her canisters.

WHAT IS BEING LEARNED

A major aspect of learning how to articulate new words is the ability to listen and notice subtle differences.

Listening well is also a requisite in the fine art of conversing!

Alphabet Trail

Here is a game your children can make with just a roll of shelving paper and colored markers. It can be rolled up to be played again another day or just used once to supply a few hours of fun both in the making and in the doing.

Two or more people

MATERIALS

shelving paper
colored markers
Optional: 26 sheets of paper; tape

DIRECTIONS

On a long roll of paper (or even twenty-six sheets of paper taped together), have the children write out the letters of the alphabet starting with A. They can use different-color markers and make letters in different patterns. Some could have polka dots, some could have stripes, some might be checkered, others could have rainbows. Lay the finished product down on the floor and play these games:

- Jump or hop forward, backward, or sideways from letter to letter in order.

- Sing the "alphabet song" as they jump, coordinating each letter they sing with the letter that is stepped or jumped on.

- Start on one letter and jump to a letter named, such as from A to F.

- Start at A and walk to the letter named with eyes closed (to see if they can remember how far each letter is from A).

- Guess how many steps it takes to get from one letter to another. For example, how many steps will it take to go from G to X? After they guess, have them walk it to see if they are right.

- Jump to the letters of the child's name or any other word.

VARIATION

Challenge your children to think of their own variations.

WHAT IS BEING LEARNED

Learning the order of the alphabet with their bodies gives children a stronger internal awareness of this sequence than just memorizing it with their mind would. There are plenty of times in life when we need to remember the order of the alphabet, such as looking up names in a phone book or words in a dictionary. Many of us have to resort to quietly singing the "alphabet song" to ourselves to remember if J comes before or after L. Having a stronger internal sense means you just know it!

People Pencils

If you have a physically active child who doesn't like sitting down with a pencil and paper to practice writing letters, this is the game for you. In

Two or more people

this game, the child is the pencil and you are the writer, or vice versa. The pencil as well as the writer has its own intelligence.

DIRECTIONS

One player stands behind the other. The player in back is the "writer" and the player in front is the "pencil." The writer uses the pencil to write a letter by moving the pencil forward and back and sideways as needed. The writer should start and stop the letter in the same way it would be done with a pencil on paper. It helps if the writer announces before each turn if he is making a capital or small letter or using cursive or block letters. When the writer is done, the pencil guesses what letter he wrote.

For more advanced players, the writer could write three or more letters in a row to make a word, and the pencil has to guess the word. If the pencil is especially clever, the writer could try writing a sentence!

VARIATIONS

♦ People Paper: With the tip of one finger, the writer writes a letter (or word or sentence) on the other player's back in the same way it would be written on paper. The paper has to guess what the letter (or word or sentence) is.

♦ People, Paper, and Board: While the writer is writing the letter on the paper's back, have the paper print the letter on a chalkboard or paper *at the same time.*

WHAT IS BEING LEARNED

The pencil is learning kinesthetically, inside his body, what a letter "feels" like. The nerves in his muscles and joints send signals to his brain that an A, for example, first moves diagonally one way and then diagonally the opposite way. Like riding a bicycle, things learned by the body are learned forever.

Finger Letters

Can you spell words with your fingers? In American Sign Language, there is a specific shape you can make with one hand to sign each letter of the alphabet. This alphabet, along with word signing, is fun to learn and useful to know. My daughters and I have used it when snorkeling and to send messages to each other across the room at parties ("Let's go now").

It's also fun to make up your own letter signs, as in this game.

DIRECTIONS

Take turns with your child forming letters with your fingers. The other player has to guess which letter is being formed.

WHAT IS BEING LEARNED

Children learn to think about the components that make up each letter: Where does it curve? Where is it straight?

They also get experience in controlling the little muscles in their hands and get a chance to be creative in their thinking.

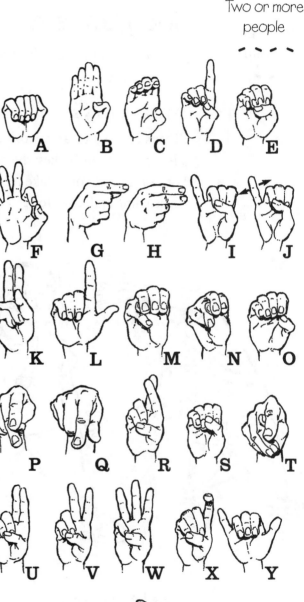

Body Letters

Writing doesn't have to be a solitary activity. In this active game, every-one can play!

DIRECTIONS

Players can form teams, work with partners, or work individually to form a letter with their bodies; the other players have to guess what the letter is. For example, it could take four children to make the letter E: one for the vertical line and three for each of the horizontal lines.

VARIATIONS

Without telling anyone what letter she has in mind, a player arranges other players to form a letter. The players who are the letter have to guess what the letter is.

A more advanced group can use body letters to form words. They can make one letter at a time or, if there are enough players, a whole word at once. Players might need to lie down to form some letters; other letters might require players to kneel, sit, or stand.

WHAT IS BEING LEARNED

All the muscles in the body get involved in this game—an excellent way to learn how to make letters and words with your whole self!

Compounding Your Words

Group
activity

I was once invited to be part of a symposium in which there were many presenters. The rooms for each presentation were really part of a much larger room, but separated by thin partitions. I was unaware of the lack of noise barriers, and our group played and laughed and giggled as usual.

Months later I wanted to present a workshop at a conference in New Mexico and I called a university professor whose name I was given as a possible contact. I didn't know her but it turned out that she immediately knew me. She said, "I was at that symposium in the room next to yours and I kept hearing everyone having a good time and wished I had chosen that workshop!"

She gave me the job as a conference presenter.

Laughter brings rewards of all kinds. Learning while having fun is a reward of its own, and this game, one of the ones we played that day, always brings giggles.

MATERIALS

list of compound words
paper
pen or pencil

DIRECTIONS

Players break up into teams of small groups or partners. Each team is given a slip of paper with a compound word, such as "windmill" or "paperback," written on it. The groups take a little time to work out a way to mime the two parts of the word. For example, partners can each do one part of the word. When all of the teams are prepared, they sit down. Then one by one the teams act out their compound words for the other players to guess.

Here are some conventional ideas for compound words you can use: doorknob, mailbox, redwood, chalkboard, seashore, flashlight, waterfall, seashell, butterfly, raincoat, grasshopper, flytrap, bathtub, mousetrap, knothole, airplane, teacup, dragonfly, rainbow, teardrop, paintbrush, toothbrush, staircase, snowfall, snowman, carpool, moonbeam, sweatshirt, armchair

WHAT IS BEING LEARNED

Children learn that some larger words are made up of two smaller words, which helps them decode larger words.

This game also teaches bigger things. One is how to use one's creativity to find a way to convey a message to others nonverbally (a particularly useful skill when traveling to countries where you do not speak the language).

Children also gain experience in getting up and performing in front of others. Being the center of attention and having all eyes focus on you is one of the most stressful situations we face. But succeeding at public speaking is also one of the top self-esteem boosters. There is almost nothing more satisfying than knowing you went out there in front of everyone and pulled it off! Acting out a compound word gives players a brief and doable amount of time to be the "star" and feel the glow of success.

Window Shade Rhyming Games

I was looking through our office closet for a large sheet of paper. I thought I saw some rolled up in there. Instead I found a broken window shade and I thought, "Perfect! Now this game that teaches rhyming words doesn't have to be a one- or two-time game that gets worn out from the jumping and hopping. It can be neatly rolled up and played time and time again."

If you don't have a window shade, use a roll of shelf paper or poster board. They are pretty sturdy, too.

MATERIALS

window shade, roll of paper, or poster board
crayons, paint, or felt-tip markers

DIRECTIONS

On the window shade or paper, draw the letters of the alphabet. Ask each player to jump or hop to the letter that starts the word "fat." Then ask her to jump to other letters that start words that rhyme with "fat."

Here are suggestions for other simple rhyming words:

AT words: fat, cat, mat, bat, sat, hat

AN words: can, fan, pan, man, tan, van, ran

AP words: tap, rap, sap, lap, map, cap, nap

AG words: rag, nag, bag, sag, wag, tag, hag, gag, zag

AD words: bad, pad, mad, dad, had, sad

AM words: Sam, ham, ram, jam, Pam, yam

IN words: fin, win, bin, pin, kin, tin

IP words: dip, hip, lip, nip, rip, sip, tip, yip, zip

EN words: den, hen, men, pen, ten, yen

UG words: bug, dug, hug, jug, lug, mug, pug, rug, tug

UT words: but, cut, gut, hut, jut, nut, rut

UN words: bun, fun, nun, pun, run, sun

OG words: bog, cog, dog, fog, hog, jog, log

OT words: cot, dot, got, hot, jot, lot, not, pot, rot

IP words: dip, hip, lip, nip, rip, sip, tip, yip, zip

IT words: bit, fit, hit, kit, nit, pit, sit, wit

EG words: beg, leg, peg

ET words: bet, set, let, get, jet, met, net, pet, wet, yet

OP words: cop, hop, mop, pop, top

WHAT IS BEING LEARNED

Rhyming, phonics, and the order of the alphabet are all being reinforced in this game. If you have the children hop instead of jump, they are also getting practice in balance because hopping on one foot requires a weight shift and a realignment of the body to find a new center of balance.

All Ages

Hot Ball/Cold Ball

Group activity

Tossing a ball back and forth with a group of children can easily become monotonous. You can spice up the game and recharge the energy by changing the way the ball is tossed. I call this game Hot Ball/Cold Ball, and that's only two of the ways. . . .

MATERIALS

ball or something that can be thrown

DIRECTIONS

One person gets to be Caller, and this person explains beforehand what each call will mean. The Caller is allowed to make up new variations, if wanted.

The players form a circle and toss the ball around from person to person.

When the Caller yells out "hot ball," the players toss the ball *overhand* to each other as quickly as possible.

If the Caller says "cold ball," the players toss the ball gently and slowly *underhand* to each other until the next command is given.

If the Caller says "crooked ball," the player has to *lift a leg* and toss the ball under the leg to another player.

If the Caller says "twirly ball," the player has to *twirl around* before throwing the ball. (There could be a "hot twirly ball" as well as a "cold twirly ball.")

If the Caller says "sound ball," the thrower has to *make a sound* before throwing the ball.

Advanced players could have calls like "sound hot twirly ball," where the players would catch the ball, twirl around, make a sound, and throw it quickly overhand!

VARIATIONS

There are many possibilities in instructions, and there are also different possibilities in the type of ball chosen. A tennis ball presents a different game than a beach ball. And who says it has to be a ball? Rolled-up socks or a knotted scarf could work, too, making this a game that can be spontaneously played anywhere and anytime.

WHAT IS BEING LEARNED

Learning to really listen is a skill that can't be overrated. We have all had the experience of hearing someone talking to us but a few minutes later realizing that we don't know was said. Our ears can hear but if our brain is not simultaneously engaged, we aren't listening.

Hot Ball/Cold Ball motivates players to keep their ears open, minds active, and bodies alert because after they hears the call, they must act on it!

Group
activity

Category Toss

This game can be made very simple for the young ones, more complicated for the school-age kids, and fun for the whole family.

Perhaps you've played a similar game in your youth when everyone in the circle starts doing a clapping, snapping pattern and then takes turns naming examples of a category, such as flowers or cities. The idea in that game was to keep the rhythm and only name the example when you snapped your fingers.

This version is easier. You just have to toss a ball.

MATERIALS

ball, beanbag, or anything easy to catch

DIRECTIONS

The players sit in a circle, although this game can also be played with just two people.

Decide on a category, such as types of flowers, types of trees, names of friends, names that start with a certain letter, favorite foods, names of shapes, names of planets, names of states, names of countries, things made out of wood, types of furniture, and so on.

For example, let's say the category is movies. Give the first player a ball or beanbag. The first player names a movie and then tosses the ball to another player, who names another movie. The ball is tossed until every player has had a turn or until no one can think of any more examples.

VARIATIONS

The variations of themes for this game are endless.

You can play this game with a group who are just getting acquainted; it's a way the members can learn more about each other. The categories can be places I've visited, places I want to visit, food I love, food I hate, sports I play, sports I watch, television shows I never miss, movies that made me cry, and so on.

You can also vary the way the ball is passed. It can be rolled, kicked, or bounced or you can make up a rule, such as the ball has to be thrown with the right hand but caught with the left.

What is thrown can also vary. The ball can be a large fitness ball or a beach ball or a tennis ball, or it can be something easier to catch, such as a scarf or a beanbag or a stuffed teddy bear.

WHAT IS BEING LEARNED

Children get experience in naming and understanding categories. They also get practice in sharpening their listening and memory skills. They need to pay attention to what examples were already said, so they don't repeat them. Categorizing is a more advanced version of matching. Instead of noticing only similarities between two things, the players become aware of similarities among a group of things.

Dictionary Game

Group
activity

My daughter Marissa introduced this game to us at a family gathering. It was such fun and only required a dictionary and some creativity.

People of all ages can learn new words. One of the words I took was "schadenfreude," which means getting pleasure from the misfortune of others (described in the dictionary as "malicious joy"). I never heard the word before, but the very next day I was reading Time *magazine and there it was in an article. Funny how that happens.*

MATERIALS

dictionary

pencils

paper

DIRECTIONS

Each player takes a turn looking through the dictionary to find a word that he has never heard of before and suspects that no one else has, either.

Once each player has a word and has written the correct definition on a piece of paper, the games begin.

One person says his new word and all the other players write down a definition. Since usually no one has a clue as to the real definition, the trick is to write down something that sounds likely and will fool the others.

Then the person who knows the real meaning gathers up the slips of papers, including the real definition, and reads them all out loud. The other players individually vote on which one they think is the true definition.

If you want to keep score, the player who fools someone with a phony definition gets a point for each person tricked. Any players who guess the correct definition get three points.

We also gave a point to the person who wrote the goofiest pretend definition if it made us laugh.

VARIATION

Play the same game without writing or giving points. Just take turns finding words in the dictionary and everyone tries to figure out the meaning.

WHAT IS BEING LEARNED

All who play this game enlarge their vocabularies. They also get to expand their creativity by making up definitions.

But, maybe more important, the game gives the players an enjoyable way to be together using something as simple as a dictionary.

‘ ⌒ ‿ ⌒ ‿ ⌒ ‿ ﹀

PART THREE

Games That Enhance Math Skills

Mathematical skills include the ability to mentally process logical prob-lems and equations, as well as to understand numbers and their rela-tionship to each other. Math skills are probably the most popularly understood of the cognitive skills and the ones most often found on multiple-choice standardized tests. Individuals who have high mathematical abilities are able to do complicated math problems and process logical questions at a rapid rate.

All of these skills sound impressive but they need to start somewhere. At the first level of mathmatical learning, children need to be able to count, to recognize numbers, to estimate, to add, to subtract, and to understand sim-ple concepts, such as that 1 stands for one unit and 2 for two units.

These games use the unusual—drama, breath, straws, and Kung Fu(!)—to teach children these basics.

AGES 6 AND UNDER

Straw Counts

This ridiculously simple activity will keep your toddler occupied and focused for a much longer time than you'd expect. I am always surprised at the different ages who want to play this simple game of putting pieces of straw into a bottle. It must satisfy a deep urge in all of us to start a task and see it so neatly come to completion.

When you sit down and play this game with your little one, you can count each straw that gets put in the bottle and reinforce the memorizing aspect of counting.

MATERIALS

   scissors
   straws
   empty 8-ounce (250 ml) plastic water bottle

DIRECTIONS

Cut up some straws into small pieces. The size of the pieces depends on the age of your child. The pieces need to be big enough that they can't be swallowed and small enough so they don't bend easily. For toddlers, I cut them about an inch or two in length.

Take the lid off the top of the bottle and show your little one how she can put each straw piece into the hole. Have her count each piece as she drops it in.

As your learner becomes more adept at this skill, increase the challenge by poking a small hole in the lid just large enough to fit the straw pieces through and put the lid back on the bottle.

VARIATION

Have your child drop buttons into an empty oatmeal or salt container. Make a slit at the top for the buttons to go through. Or you can have her count pennies as she drops them into a piggy bank.

However, note that with the above materials, you need to watch that the child doesn't put the objects in her mouth. With straws, it is possible to cut them long enough that they don't present a choking hazard.

WHAT IS BEING LEARNED

In addition to practice in learning to count, children get early experience in eye-hand coordination. Their eyes direct their hands to put the straw into the bottle. They'll soon learn that if their eyes are looking somewhere else, the straw will miss going into the hole.

Also, it's another opportunity for children to practice focusing their attention on a task and completing it, a skill they are going to need their whole life long.

You Can with Cans

Two or more people

Aluminum cans are easy to collect and great for games. Try this fun bowling and counting game before you recycle your cans to get double the use out of each can. But if you want the excitement without the noise, use empty plastic water bottles instead of aluminum cans.

MATERIALS

empty aluminum cans or plastic water bottles
beach ball or beanbag or other ball

DIRECTIONS

Stack a few cans on top of each other or set up six to ten cans in a pyramid shape as if they were bowling pins. Have your player stand two to six

feet away, depending on his skill level, and roll a
beach ball at the cans. Count how many
cans fall down. Take as many turns as
needed to knock down all of the cans.
Have the child help you set up the
cans again for the next round.

If you don't have a beach ball or
another rubber ball handy, use a beanbag that players can toss at a stack of
cans. If you don't have a beanbag
handy, make your own by putting
some dried beans in the toe of a
sock and tying the top into a knot.

VARIATIONS

Cover each can with some paper and write a number on each can. Line
the cans up and ask your player to aim for can number 2, for example. Or,
for the very new learners, simply exclaim their achievements: "Look, you
knocked over the number 2 can and the number 5 can!"

For the older learners, write down the numbers that got knocked down
and have your player add them up. "Let's see, you knocked down number 3,
number 4, and number 7. Let's figure out what your score is for this round."

If you have children of various ages, you can assign them different tasks
or have them take turns; for example, the younger one can name the number, the older one can do the adding, and the middle one (the one who
already knows his numbers but it not ready for addition problems) can stack
the cans back up for the next round. Kids like to have titles, so the person
who does the adding is King Counter, the person who stacks the can is Sir
Stacker, and the person who throws the ball is Major Thrower.

WHAT IS BEING LEARNED

Children are learning eye-hand coordination and figuring out how much
force is needed to knock many cans down at the same time. They are learning how to count the number of cans that they knock over. They are also

learning to help each other by stacking the cans after each game and the coordination it takes to stack or line up the cans.

If you play the variations, children also learn about number recognition and addition. If they are asked to set up the numbered cans in order, they are also learning the order of numbers.

Two or more people

Cereal Necklace

Stringing things, such as beads for a necklace, requires the fine motor skill of finger manipulation. In this stringing activity, children will also count their "beads" when they are done. But the best part is that children can munch on their finished necklace all day long.

MATERIALS

yarn, string, or fishing line
cereal that has holes in the middle

DIRECTIONS

Give your child a piece of yarn, string, or fishing line that is long enough to fit over her head when tied, and have her string pieces of cereal on the yarn.

If you use yarn or string, it can be helpful to younger ones to put a piece of tape on the stringing end so that it's firmer and goes more easily through the hole in the cereal. Tie the ends of the yarn together when she's done to make a necklace.

Have your child count how many pieces of cereal are on the string. Later in the day, before the cereal has all been eaten, count how many pieces are left. Can your child figure out how many were eaten?

VARIATIONS

If you want your necklace to be lasting, instead of edible, string other things, such as buttons, short pieces of colored straws, or macaroni and other hollow pasta shapes.

Instead of string or yarn, you could use pipe cleaners and turn the project into rings for the fingers or loops to hang around the ears.

WHAT IS BEING LEARNED

Children get practice in counting and begin to get an idea of the concept of subtraction. In this case, instead of "take aways," it is "eaten aways."

Children also get an opportunity to practice their fine motor control.

Guess Who? Guess What?

One or two
people

Can you look at a little section of a picture and then guess what the whole picture is? That's the challenge in this game. Take turns with your child being the guesser or have a group of children pair up and take turns choosing pictures and guessing.

MATERIALS

scissors
paper
magazine

DIRECTIONS

Cut a piece of paper into horizontal strips, leaving the left-hand margin intact so that the strips are still attached to the paper. This will be your picture cover.

Place the picture cover over one of the magazine pictures and pull back the strips, one by one, and see if your player can guess what the picture is about. Change places and let the player pick out a picture for you to guess.

By taking along this page of strips in a magazine, you'll have an instant game for passing time in waiting rooms or when traveling.

VARIATION

Use photos of someone your child knows and see if she can identify the person.

WHAT IS BEING LEARNED

Children are learning an early mathmatical concept that a whole is made up of smaller parts. In this game, they see that a whole picture is made up of separate parts and that each part is necessary.

It would be nice to get this concept understood on a global scale so that each of us would realize that everyone is a necessary part of the whole.

AGES 6 AND UP

One or two people

Breath Math

This game of counting and subtracting focuses on the breath. It has the nice side effect of calming, and children can always benefit from that.

DIRECTIONS

Using a stopwatch or timer to mark one minute, have each player count the number of inhalations and exhalations he takes during that minute.

Then ask the players to run around the room, or do jumping jacks or some other aerobic activity, for two to three minutes to get their heart rates up.

Now have the players stop and count their breath again.

Have the players subtract the smaller rate from the larger and see the difference.

VARIATION

While sitting quietly, ask the players to count their breaths for one minute. Then ask them to consciously slow their breathing and feel completely relaxed. After five or ten minutes, count the number of inhales and exhales in one minute again and compare the rate to the previous number.

WHAT IS BEING LEARNED

Little children are practicing their counting and their awareness that the number 1 means one unit of something and 2 means two units, and so on.

Children who are a bit older are getting a chance to understand and use subtraction skills in a meaningful way.

All children are learning that they have some control over their bodies. Even though we think our breathing is an unconscious involuntary reflex, we can see that we can affect our breath with our movements and with our stillness.

Kung Fu Math

Two or more people

"Teach us Kung Fu!" a group of adolescent boys once shouted in Spanish at my colleague Sandy. Sandy didn't know Kung Fu from Fuji apples, but since she had Asian features, they assumed she did.

We were at a large orphanage called Nuestros Hermanos Pequenos (Our Little Brothers) in Honduras, where Sandy and I were to give a workshop on ways to teach academics using movement games.

Sandy explained that she didn't know Kung Fu but the boys weren't having any of that. They wanted to learn now! She gave up protesting and lined the boys up in a row facing her. First, she bowed to them in her best Far Eastern manner and they bowed back. Then she taught them the only move she knew: the hitch kick, where you hop on one foot and then kick the other one up as high as you can. She held up her hand to give the boys a height to aim for. After the practice, the math game began.

DIRECTIONS

Ask each player in turn to solve a simple math problem. Math problems should vary in difficulty depending on the player's age. For example, young children could tackle four plus three or ten minus two, and older children could be given problems that require multiplying or dividing.

Once the player figures out the correct answer (with a little help from friends, if needed), he answers it by doing the hitch kick that many times across the room.

VARIATION

Instead of using only karate moves, you can use ballet or other dance steps and children could answer the math problems using only movement: "How much is six divided by three? Show me the answer in the number of pirouettes." "How many cha cha turns does it take to answer the problem eight divided by two?"

WHAT IS BEING LEARNED

Children are more attentive about doing math problems when they use movements to provide the answers. Young bodies love to move. If you know more karate moves or a repertoire of different movements, your children can also be learning about marital arts or dance steps.

Math Story

As any good lecturer will tell you, if you want your audience to remember your point, make it into a story. The same goes for teaching concepts to children. They are more likely to understand and remember if they see, hear, or act it out in story form. Use this story to help children understand addition and subtraction—or make up one of your own!

If you're doing this at home where you don't have a classroom of children to use as "props," use something else, such as dolls, action figures, paper cutouts, or fingers.

DIRECTIONS

Start the story with one person and then keep adding others to teach about addition. This story is partly based on something my daughter Roxanne came up with when she was seven and was going to a new school the next day. Having a strategy calmed her new-school jitters and helped her fall asleep.

Once upon a time there was one girl named Anna who was going to a new school. She didn't know anyone there and she was worried that she wouldn't have any friends to play with.

So, she came up with this plan:

If she made only one friend (bring one child up to join "Anna") and that new friend had a friend (add another child), then Anna would have two new friends. Let's count them—1, 2.

Now, if that second friend also had a friend (another child enters), then Anna would have three friends. Let's count them—1, 2, 3.

If that third friend already had a friend (add another child), then Anna would have four friends. Let's count them—1, 2, 3, 4.

And so on and so on depending on how high you want your learner to practice and how many children (or dolls) you have. You can end by saying:

So the little girl wasn't worried anymore because she had TEN (or whatever the ending number) new friends!

You can now, if you want, introduce subtraction.

After playing awhile, one friend had to leave early to go to her dance class (one child leaves), so Anna just had three friends. Let's count them—1, 2, 3. Then another friend had to leave to go to soccer practice (another child leaves), so Anna only had two friends. Let's count them—1, 2. Then another child went home to be with her new baby sister (another child leaves). Let's count how many friends are left—1.

Anna and her new one friend played and played the rest of the day because even just one friend is pretty wonderful, too!

VARIATION

Make up any story you like that incorporates numbers.

You also can also act out songs the children know, such as:

> Ten little monkeys jumping on the bed
> One falls off and bumps his head
> The mommy called the doctor and the doctor said
> No more monkeys jumping on the bed
> Nine little monkeys jumping on the bed
> (repeat above verse and keep subtracting monkeys until)
> No more monkeys jumping on the bed.

For slightly older children, they or you can make up a story that involves larger numbers. (Sixteen trombone players met six monkeys playing drums and two aardvarks playing banjos. How big a band did they make?)

WHAT IS BEING LEARNED

Children can count from one to ten at a very young age, but it doesn't mean they understand the concept of one being one thing and two being two things, and so on. Acting out these kinds of stories makes the concept real and introduces the concepts of addition and subtraction.

Counting on Estimates

How many jelly beans are in the jar? How many people were at the party? There are many situations in our lives in which we use our ability to estimate. In this game, we give children some experience in estimating.

Two or more
people

MATERIALS

a bowl of large dried beans, or similar objects

DIRECTIONS

Put a bowl of dried beans on the table. Players grab some with their hands and keep the beans in a fist in front of them. Then, without looking at the number of beans in their own or the other people's hands, each player makes a guess about how many beans are in everyone's hands all together.

Or they could just guess if the total number of beans in everyone's hands is an odd or even number.

One player then counts up the beans to see who guessed the correct total (or is closest to the correct number), or who was right about it being an odd or even amount.

If there are only a few players, children can learn to be sly and pretend to take a handful but only take a few—"the hand is faster than the eye" kind of trick.

VARIATIONS

◆ Players can guess how many beans there are in the whole bowl and then take them out and count them and see whose guess comes closest.

Instead of beans, you can use buttons or coins. I guess you could use small candies, but the game could get more and more frantic as the sugar rush kicks in. Hard candies might be better, because it takes awhile to suck on one.

♦ Encourage children to estimate the amounts of other things in their lives. For example, they could guess how many steps there are before they walk up them. (If it's a long flight of stairs, guessing and then counting can make the climbing more of a game and less overwhelming.) Guess how many windows there are in the room or pictures on the wall. This is a good way to spend the time when you are waiting somewhere and you need to amuse each other.

WHAT IS BEING LEARNED

Children are learning to count. They are learning to make educated guesses about amounts. They are also learning what even and odd numbers are.

Group activity

A Number of Number Ways

The great thing about this game is that there are a number of ways to play it so that different ages and skill levels can play together. Each player gets his or her own challenge and everyone wins.

MATERIALS

colored markers

paper

tape

"gentle ball" such as a beanbag or a ball made out of newspaper (see other ideas for gentle balls under Gentle Ball Games, p. 125)

DIRECTIONS

There is a simple way to do this game if you are playing with just a few children and a more elaborate way if you are playing with a larger group.

Here's the simpler way. See the variation section for the more elaborate way.

Write the numbers from 0 to 9 on separate pieces of paper. Use different colored markers so that you have, for example, a red 1, a blue 2, a green 3, and so on.

Tape the numbers in different spots on a wall.

Give the first player a ball, such as a beanbag or a ball made out of newspaper, and instruct her to use the ball to hit a certain number. Your directions should vary depending on the player's age or skill level.

Here are some suggestions for directions:

♦ Throw the ball at the red (blue, green, etc.) number.

♦ Throw the ball at the number 4 (6, 2, 5, etc.).

♦ Throw the ball at an even number.

♦ Throw the ball at an odd number.

♦ Throw the ball at the numbers that make 24.

♦ Throw the ball at the numbers that make 240.

♦ Throw the ball at the number that is the total of 2 plus 3.

♦ Throw the ball at the number that results from 5 minus 3.

♦ Throw the ball at the number that is the answer to 2 times 3.

♦ Throw the ball at the number that is the answer to 6 divided by 3.

♦ Throw the ball at the number that is the same as the Roman number IV.

♦ Throw the ball at the numbers that make 3,447.

♦ Memorize this sequence of colors—red, green, blue. Throw the ball at those three colors in order.

♦ Memorize this sequence of numbers—2-7-4-9. Throw the ball at those four numbers in order.

♦ Throw the ball at the square root of 4.

Once the children get the idea, they can start making up challenges for each other. Let big sister make up a direction for her baby brother

("Louie, go take this ball and touch it on that red number . . . over there near the couch.")

VARIATIONS

This way is considered more elaborate not only because it involves more players, but also because it requires more preparation and adds the factor of "danger" by putting the kids behind the targets.

Cut up cardboard boxes into separate pieces of cardboard. As in the game above, mark a number on each piece of cardboard using colored markers so each number is a different color.

Each child, except for the player with the ball, holds one piece of cardboard in front of his or her body. The children stand side by side facing the player with the ball.

Using the suggestions above, give each player a direction. If, for example, you say, "Throw the ball at the number that is the total of 2 plus 3," both the person throwing the ball and the person holding the cardboard that has the number 5 on it need to know that the answer is 5. The person

holding the 5 needs to know because when the ball comes at her, she may need to use her cardboard to protect herself from getting hit.

Getting hit with a "gentle ball" doesn't hurt. If some children throw a mean fastball, don't discourage them. Throwing hard and fast is a good skill. Put a paper or carpet square to mark the spot where that thrower stands. For the fast thrower, move that spot back a few feet. Move it closer for a child whose throw is less robust. Children don't mind when I move some closer and others farther away. I might say something like "And this is your spot. And here's yours . . ." Everyone is aware that some are stronger than others.

I find that children enjoy this game because it's a thrilling, and maybe more memorable, way to practice their math skills than sitting at their desks writing out answers. I find that students are much more willing to do math if it involves big movements!

If you'd rather play this game without any "danger" of getting hit with a ball, cut the cardboard boxes in a way that three sections are intact, forming screens that will stand on their own.

Set the screens up in front of the players, and let each child take turns throwing.

If a child throws the ball at the wrong number, don't make a big deal about it. Just point out something positive, such as "Good throwing. Nice try." Or "You got the idea but here's the number 4 over here. Throw it at this number. Right on!"

Or you can tape the numbers to the floor and give the children the same kinds of questions, but instead of throwing at the correct answer, they jump on it.

WHAT IS BEING LEARNED

This game is a way of presenting math lessons disguised as fun. The children who throw are practicing their eye-hand coordination and learning that if they look where they throw, they will be more accurate. The children behind the shield also gain valuable skills. They are practicing focusing, that is, paying attention to the moment. They are learning how to judge a ball's speed and trajectory in order to anticipate where it is going and what body part they need to shield. The feedback as to whether they are correct is immediate!

ALL AGES

Mr. Clock, Mr. Clock

If you don't already know this game, you'll be glad to learn it. It is always a giant success with the little ones, and even with the big ones whom you'd think would be too old to play. This general appeal makes it an ideal game to play with a mixed-age group. Try it at the next birthday party or family reunion. You'll be a big hit.

DIRECTIONS

A group of players stands at one end of a large room or field and one person stands at the other. This lone person is Mr. Clock or Ms. Clock, as the case may be.

The group yells, "Mr. Clock, Mr. Clock, what time is it?" And Mr. Clock says, "Ten o'clock" (or any time he wants). Then the group, together, counts out ten steps, walking toward Mr. Clock. The group then repeats the question, and Mr. Clock keeps giving different times until the group is very near to him. At any point then, Mr. Clock can respond, "MIDNIGHT," which is everyone's cue to run like mad back to the starting line with Mr. Clock hot in pursuit. Everyone tagged by Mr. Clock joins his side and also becomes Mr. Clock. The game continues until all but one person has been tagged. That person becomes the new Mr. Clock for the next game.

I find that when there is a group of Mr. Clocks, the children should take turns calling out the time; otherwise the loudest child will always call out the time, and the most excited child will yell out "midnight" while the group is still too far away to tag. If I am on the Mr. Clock side, I touch the shoulder of the next person to call out the time. If that person says something like "five-thirty," we figure that means five and a half steps!

VARIATION

Instead of Mr. Clock, there could be Mr. Wolf, Mr. Kangaroo, or Mr. Tiger. Children playing with Mr. Kangaroo could jump for each number instead of taking steps. Children playing with Mr. Tiger might do leaps. The running signal word could be changed from "MIDNIGHT" to "DINNER-TIME!"

WHAT IS BEING LEARNED

The main lesson here is that each number stands for that many steps; numbers are not just words for children to memorize but actually stand for something concrete.

The children who become Mr. Clock learn about waiting for the proper time to call out "midnight," which may be their first experience in long-range planning!

And best of all, it's a great reason to run.

How Many Steps?

*Walking from one place to another can sometimes be a big chore when
you are with little ones. They might like to dawdle, get distracted, or feel
overwhelmed by the distance they need to cover and refuse to budge. This
game helps children stay focused and moving.*

*I must admit that I play this game myself sometimes when I'm not in
the mood to walk as far as I need to, even when I have no child with me.*

DIRECTIONS

Guess how many steps you will need to take to get from one spot to another.
For smaller children, break up the goal into little stages. How many steps
from here to the corner? Then, how many steps from the corner to the fire
hydrant? Players guess and then see how many steps it actually does take.

Players can count individually, but it's fun to count together.

For older children, everyone playing makes a guess about how many
steps they will need to walk for longer distances; for example, the three
blocks to the parking lot. Is it a 400-step walk or only 150? The more you
play the game, the better you get at estimating.

With older children, you can also figure out how many of the child's
footsteps make a foot, then calculate how many feet (or meters) they
walked. How many yards is that?

VARIATIONS

If you are somewhere alone or don't mind appearing a bit silly, you can
say "How many giant steps?" or "How many baby (heel-to-toe) steps?"
and try walking that way. Not only is this style distracting, it also reinforces
for little ones the difference between large and small.

You can also play this game in the house just for the fun of it. How
many steps do you think there are between the front door and the back?
How many baby steps? How many giant steps? What takes more steps, the

distance between the couch and the kitchen table or between the easy chair and the closet?

WHAT IS BEING LEARNED

Children are learning to estimate lengths and distance and to develop an internal sense of length and distance. Younger children get practice in counting, and everyone learns a way of making a long walk seem shorter.

Palm Measuring

Two or more people

Measuring began before tape measures or rulers were invented. Many different cultures used body parts to measure things, which, of course, is why we still measure in feet. There are still times when measuring with your body comes in handy, such as when you're wondering "Will this table fit into that space beside the couch?" Introducing your children to the art of palm measuring gives them a good start in understanding measurements and a "handy" solution for those times when a measuring tape isn't available.

DIRECTIONS

Show your child or children how things can be measured according to the size of the palm of their hand. How many palms long is a desk, a book, a pencil? Have the players estimate how many palms long something will be, and then have them measure it with their palms to see how accurate their guess was. Note that if a hand is larger, it will take fewer palms and be a different palm measurement.

VARIATIONS

♦ Use other parts of the body, such as a finger or a foot, to measure. Walk heel to toe to measure the size of a room or the distance from one piece of furniture to another in "feet."

♦ Measure each player's palm, foot, or finger with a tape measure and then figure out the actual measurements of the things you measured above.

♦ Instead of using body parts, use movements to measure a space. For example, how many jumps does it take to go from one end of the room to the other or from the door to the table?

Always have players estimate the answer ahead of time.

WHAT IS BEING LEARNED

Children are learning an easy way to measure things. They are also seeing the connection between the abstract world of measuring ("It's ten feet long") and the actual concrete experience.

They are also getting experiences in guessing and estimating. Estimating elicits involvement in the activity because we all like to know if we are right or get of sense of how close we were so we'll be right the next time.

Group
activity

Beach Ball Bounce

This game is a fun and lively way to see the joys of teamwork. Only when children are working together can they control the movements of the ball on the sheet. When the children jerk the sheet up at diferent times instead of together as a group, the ball falls off. I love it when a child figures this out and says, "We need to do it together!"

MATERIALS

sheet or light blanket
beach ball

DIRECTIONS

Spread out a sheet or lightweight blanket and have all the players pick it up by holding on to the edges. Place a beach ball in the middle of the sheet and have all the players lift the sheet up simultaneously so that the ball goes up in the air. Call out the number "One!" When the ball falls back down to the sheet, the players gently jerk up the sheet again and count "Two!" Continue until the ball falls off the sheet, then start over. See if the team can keep getting to higher numbers.

Sometimes you'll find that on one try, you can't even get to five and on another your count is over 100! Challenge everyone to work together and keep getting better.

You might find, depending on the ages and sensitivity of the group, that having someone call out "one, two, three, pull up" helps the group rhythm stay smooth and in unison.

VARIATION

Don't have a beach ball handy? Try a rag doll, stuffed animal, or small pillow. Whatever it is needs to be soft in case it hits someone, and light enough that it gives a good bounce. These types of ball substitutes have an advantage in that they don't roll away when they land on the floor.

WHAT IS BEING LEARNED

Besides the social skill of working together, this game gives children practice in counting and learning that each bounce stands for one number. Children may be able to count to ten or even a hundred and still not understand that 4, for example, stands for four separate things. This game provides another way to understand the real meaning of numbers because each number stands for the bounce of the ball.

`~ ~ ~ ~ ~`

PART FOUR

Games That Enhance Kinesthetic Skills

Kinesthetic skills are those that involve having control of the body's movements, including balance, agility, grace, and a sense of how one's body should act and react in any physical situation. Some individuals are natural athletes and have strong bodily skills even before formal training. However, all of us, no matter where we start, can improve our kinesthetic skills with practice and varied experiences.

Children who are strong in their kinesthetic intelligence need to move. They love to touch and learn best by doing. They are adept at activities that involve gross and fine motor activities, such as sports, dance, arts, crafts, theater, fixing mechanical things, and using the computer.

From birth, children need to learn about their bodies and how to move them. We can help them with this process, using nothing fancier than such things as a balloon, a tube sock, a blanket, some toothpicks, and ourselves.

Many of the easy games listed can be played with just you and your little one. Many of them can be played with you and anyone else who wants to join in. We all benefit from learning to move our bodies well.

AGES 6 AND UNDER

Human Hoop

One or two people

Tossing the ball around with Dad in the backyard must be high on the list of all-time-great childhood moment for any child who has had this experience. But there is more than one way to play ball. If your child isn't quite ready for the major leagues, try this variation of ball playing. It can be done with little ones and it can be done indoors on a rainy day.

MATERIALS

newspaper

"gentle ball," such as a beanbag or a bunched-up newspaper (see ideas for types of gentle balls in Gentle Ball Games, p. 125)

DIRECTIONS

Lay down a newspaper for the foul line and become a human basketball hoop for your child by using your arms to form a large circle. Encourage your player to throw the ball in the "hoop" from the foul line. Move slowly around the room to ensure that she gets some throws in from all sides. (This also gives her some practice in using her eyes for scanning.)

Of course, you may sometimes get hit in the face by those "rim shots," but no one said parenting would be free of occupational hazards! To minimize danger, I encourage children to toss gently underhand for this game.

If the thrower is a little less skilled, she can still be successful if the human hoop is clever enough to move quickly into the right position to give the ball a clean shot.

VARIATIONS

If you have a full skirt on or a large shirt, hold it out in front of you and use that as the basketball hoop. Other possible "hoops" include holding a basket, a wastebasket, a milk carton cut in half, a plastic gallon bottle cut in half with the handle left on, and an upside-down traffic cone.

WHAT IS BEING LEARNED

This is an opportunity for children to practice their eye-hand coordination, but it also has another advantage: In this game of basketball, both the thrower and the basket can be active.

Jolly Jumps

One or two people

If you want a fast distraction for a grumpy child or a child who is misbehaving, try this game. Distraction is the best method for dealing with a child's negative mood or to get him to do something other than what he is doing. It beats saying "no" or "don't" or "cheer up," especially since those words often produce the opposite results. And once he's jumping, it'll be hard for him not to be jolly!

DIRECTIONS

Give your child the friendly challenge: "Hey, can you jump up and turn around in the air?"

Demonstrate by jumping and giving your body a half turn so that you land facing in the opposite direction.

"Can you do a quarter turn?" (Land facing one side or another)

"How about a full turn?" (Do a complete revolution in the air before landing)

VARIATION

Once your child has the turns accomplished, add this challenge:

"Let's do a pattern. First we do a small quarter turn and from there a half turn and then finish with a full turn. Ta da!"

WHAT IS BEING LEARNED

Children are learning a skill called motor planning. They have to internally program their muscles to accomplish the plan their mind has requested. This is the same kind of skill that will help them figure out the best way to climb a tree, for example, and the safest way to get down.

Just You and Me and a Balloon

One or two people

These are sweet games to play with your munchkin when all you have is a balloon and a lovely space of time together.

MATERIALS

balloon

DIRECTIONS

Both of you sit on the floor with your hands propped behind you so that you can lift your legs. Push or gently kick the balloon back and forth between you with your feet.

Next, lie on your backs with your heads touching. Pass the balloon over your heads to each other. Then bring your feet over your head and pass the balloon to each other using only your feet to hold the balloon.

VARIATIONS

◆ Balloon Walk: Kneel so that you and your darling are eye-to-eye. Stay close so that you can snuggle the balloon between your bellies and move sideways across the room without losing the balloon.

Try other ways of moving with the balloon in between you, such as

◇ Going to the other end of the room with one person facing forward and the other backward

◇ Moving in a circle

◇ Putting the balloon in different positions, such as between your hips or heads

♦ Balloon Massage: As your little one lies on the floor, roll the balloon over her body. Use just the right amount of pressure so that she feels it and it makes her smile.

If your partner is under three, this is a good time to reinforce the names of body parts. ("Ms. Balloon is rolling over your chest . . . and now she's heading down your arms. . . . She loves your yummy body" or whatever words come to you.)

Take turns and let your sweetie roll the balloon over your body, too.

WHAT IS BEING LEARNED

The central theme of all these balloon games is being aware of one's body. Whether it's using their feet to pass the balloon or holding it against their hips or having it rolled over their tummy, the game helps children notice their various body parts and feel them working separately.

Blanket Ride

Two or more people

I first discovered this game when I was working with a child who had muscular dystrophy. I had to come up with activities that would increase his muscle tone and his balancing skills.

In his preschool class I laid a lightweight blanket down for him to sit on. As he sat on it, a classmate spontaneously (and maybe a bit mischievously) began to pull it. I joined in and pulled, too. The ride the boy got taken on was perfect for enhancing his balancing skills as he kept adjusting his trunk muscles in order to stay upright.

Then some of the other kids, seeing the fun in progress, wanted a turn. Some wanted a blanket ride. Others wanted to be the ones who pulled the

blanket, the first boy among them. As he helped pull the sliding blanket around the room, he was strengthening his muscles. Whether he was sitting for balance or tugging for strength, this activity gave me my two goals with one game!

MATERIALS

blanket or sturdy cloth

DIRECTIONS

Have your child sit on the blanket or sturdy cloth as you pull it along the floor. Purposely jiggle the blanket this way and that and slide the blanket in various unexpected directions to give your child extra balancing practice. He'll squeal and love the added movement!

If you're playing with a group, you can help provide the extra power if more children want to sit than pull. As one of the pullers, you can also keep control over the activity so it doesn't go so fast that a child gets knocked off the blanket.

VARIATION

A cardboard box can be used in this game. One child sits inside and the others push or pull it across the floor.

WHAT IS BEING LEARNED

When sitting on the blanket, children are learning to continually adjust their trunk muscles so they stay upright while being jiggled and propelled in different directions.

When pulling, children strengthen their muscles, especially in their arms and legs.

Balloon Baseball

Two or more people

I don't like to play baseball. Okay, I hate to play baseball. It is something about this little hard ball coming dangerously fast at me and I'm supposed to somehow bat it away with a skinny piece of wood or, worse, catch it. I don't like things happening that fast. So you can see why this baseball game played with a balloon instead of a ball speaks my language. It's also just right for the toddler or beginning baseball player who may, unlike me, grow up to love the sport.

MATERIALS

rolled-up newspaper, cardboard tube, tape, plastic bottle with dowel,
   or toy bat
balloon

DIRECTIONS

Make a bat out of anything handy, such as the cardboard tube inside a paper towel roll or a rolled-up section of yesterday's newspaper secured with tape. Or find something around the house that's an appropriate size and shape for a child's bat. I especially like using an empty 2-liter plastic bottle, the kind soft drinks come in. Cut a dowel to fit inside the opening of the plastic bottle. Wrap some duct tape around the dowel and bottle opening to keep it secure and, voilà, you have a nifty bat (or hockey stick or golf club).

You could, of course, also use a toy bat.

Give the bat to your player and toss the balloon at her. The slow movements of a balloon floating toward her gives her plenty of time to line up her bat, swing at the "ball," and get the satisfaction of connecting.

You or the other players then have plenty of time to catch the balloon as it leisurely floats down.

What Is Being Learned

This game is about learning that your eyes direct the movement of your hands. In this case, the movements are in slow motion, so it's easier for children to get their hands to do what they want.

If you want to get the point across to your little one, ask her to swing at the balloon when she is looking the other way and then to swing at it when looking directly at it. It will help her see the effectiveness of watching what she is doing.

Holes-in-Your-Sheet Toss

At last—a use for a worn sheet other than as a ghost costume on Halloween!

One or two people

Materials

scissors
old worn sheet
ball

Directions

Cut a hole in the middle of the sheet and hang it from something like a clothesline or the branch of a tree.

Have your child stand on one side of the sheet while you stand on the other.

Ask your child to toss the ball to you through the hole. Then you throw the ball back to him.

You could make holes of varying sizes in the sheet, so that there are extremely easy shots through large holes as well as more difficult ones through smaller holes. This also adds to the fun of the game because the person on the other side of the sheet doesn't know from which hole the ball will appear.

VARIATION

◆ Hula Aims: Hang a hula hoop and toss the ball back and forth through the hoop with your player. The hoop provides a larger visual cue to a new ball-thrower as to where to throw the ball than the sheet does.

WHAT IS BEING LEARNED

This game requires more precision than the usual toss or target game, so children learn to focus their attention and improve their eye-hand coordination. If you play the game with many holes, a player's reflex response is also sharpened because he doesn't know which hole the ball will come through.

The Bunny Game

Two or more people

Jumping as far as you can seems to be a challenge many children love. Maybe we are born with a desire to move like our animal friends, especially the bunny.

MATERIALS

tape (masking or electrical or colored)
paper
Optional: tape measure

DIRECTIONS

Tape a piece of paper down on the floor for the child to jump from. Give your child the "bunny challenge" and ask her to jump like a bunny, as far as she can, from that spot. Put a piece of tape down where she lands. Then ask her to try again and see if she can jump farther the next time (like a kangaroo, perhaps). Give her lots of tries.

If you want to add the useful lesson of how to use a tape measure, measure the distance that is jumped each time.

VARIATION

Instead of jumping from a still position, have your bunny take a running start and then jump from the spot.

WHAT IS BEING LEARNED

Children are experimenting with their balance and the use of their powerful leg muscles. Play this game a bunch of times and those muscles will get stronger and stronger.

Domino Blowing

Every parent knows about setting up dominoes in a line so that when the first one falls, it knocks down the next, which knocks down the one after that, and so on down the line. In this variation of knocking over dominoes, you teach your child how to line them up and blow them down.

One or two
people

MATERIALS

dominoes
party blower or straw

DIRECTIONS

Show your child how to set up the dominoes so that they are side by side instead of behind each other. If your child is young, start with five or six dominoes and demonstrate how to set them up. Using a straw or a party blower (the toy that you blow on one end and a piece of paper uncurls at the other end), have your child blow the dominoes down one by one.

VARIATIONS

If your child is a little older, teach him how to set up dominoes so that they are lined up behind each other in the traditional way. Have him blow at the first one so that it falls backward and watch as the rest of the dominoes fall down in sequence.

Use more and more dominoes as your learner gets better at the game, and experiment with setting the dominoes up in different patterns.

WHAT IS BEING LEARNED

Although the game is about blowing them down, the real lesson is in setting the dominoes up. Little hands need to learn precise motor control to carefully set up the dominoes side by side so none get knocked down too soon. (The level of precision needed increases when the dominoes are set up behind each other.)

Blowing adds the element of breath control as children learn how softly to blow to make only one domino fall.

Bubble-Wrap Jump

One or two people

If you buy or receive something that is wrapped in bubble wrap, your children are in luck. The prospect of jumping off a chair onto bubble wrap is so inviting to children that even the most timid are willing to try.

This jumping game will delight the players but might make you a little nuts with the noise. Just remember that it's a temporary disturbance—the bubbles will soon all be deflated. Meanwhile, your children have gained a fun opportunity to work on motor skills.

MATERIALS

bubble wrap
chair

DIRECTIONS

Place the bubble wrap on the floor in front of a chair or bench. Let the children jump off the chair and onto the wrap and hear the snap of the bubbles bursting.

They will soon learn that it requires a certain forcefulness to jump hard enough to break the bubbles.

WHAT IS BEING LEARNED

Children are developing their leg strength and body balance and, if more than one player is playing, the fairness of taking turns.

Styrofoam Hammering

One or two people

If you have access to Styrofoam blocks, the kind that are often used as packing material, and you have a little child, a small hammer, and some golf tees or nails, you have the ingredients for a very fun activity for your child.

Styrofoam blocks provide just the right amount of resistance to hold the nail upright but respond immediately to any hammer blows, so the beginner only has to hammer lightly to see results.

MATERIALS

Styrofoam block, such as from packing material
nails or golf tees
small hammer or rock

DIRECTIONS

Take a block of Styrofoam and press in the tips of the
nails or golf tees so that the heads and most of the
length protrude. Place the nails 2 to 3 inches apart.

Give your child a small toy wooden hammer, or
a tack hammer, or any hammer you feel comfortable
having her use. Or, if you don't have a small hammer, you can use a rock.

Show her how to hammer the nail into the
block (if she hasn't already immediately seen
the possibility and started
without your demonstra-
tion).

Show her how she can
pull the hammered nails
back out of the Styrofoam,
place them in another, unused
area of the block, and hammer
again.

VARIATION

You can also use these foam blocks with screws and a screwdriver.

WHAT IS BEING LEARNED

There's nothing like hammering to hammer home the concept of eye-hand
coordination. To be effective, you have to watch what you are doing!

Rare Races

Two or more
people

I find that if I want children to do what is needed, as in "We need to go home now, so go get in the car," I get better cooperation if I frame the request differently. "Let's do the Sideways Slide and see who gets to the car first," or "Let's see how fast we can get to the car walking only on our heels."

Rare Races introduces children to new possibilities for doing things that make them more fun. It's the kind of game Mary Poppins would really love!

DIRECTIONS

The next time you want your child or a group of children to go somewhere, have fun by challenging them to try a new type of movement.

Possible movement styles are:

- ◆ Toe Races—racing on tiptoes only
- ◆ Heel Races—racing on heels only
- ◆ Toe Toe, Heel Heel, Toe Toe, Heel Heel—a rhythmic variation of them both
- ◆ Squat Race—racing in a squat position
- ◆ Outside Edges—racing on the outside edges of the feet
- ◆ Inside Edges—racing on the inside edges of the feet
- ◆ Backward— running or walking facing backward
- ◆ Sideways Sliding—racing by facing sideways, leading with one leg and sliding the other leg to meet that leg
- ◆ Gallop Race—running facing forward but always leading with the same leg
- ◆ Hopping on one foot
- ◆ Hopping on the other foot
- ◆ Hopping backward

♦ Skipping forward

♦ Skipping backward

♦ And then there is my all-time favorite: holding hands and skipping together . . . (sigh)

VARIATION

Let children make up their own "How-else-could-we-get-to-the-car?" racing style.

WHAT IS BEING LEARNED

Children are learning how to add fun to an ordinary task. It's a lesson that will have long-term benefits for them and eventually the lives of their children. Imagine, the games you play today will also reap joy for your grandchildren!

On the physical level, children are learning how to control their bodies to make them move in specific ways. They are also dealing with and strengthening their sense of balance as they put their bodies through unusual movements.

Lost in Rice

One or two people

Here are some quiet games that can keep children occupied for a long time on their own and are also fun to play with others. As the children play with the rice in different ways, they will be focusing their senses of touch, sight, and hearing.

MATERIALS

bag of rice
box or bucket
small things found around the house

DIRECTIONS

Pour a bag of rice into a box or bucket. The more rice you use, the more fun it will be.

Gather up pairs of a variety of small household objects, such as spoons, paper clips, poker chips, pennies, pencils, and so on.

Bury one of each pair in the rice.

Give one item to your player to feel and ask her to find the matching item that is hidden in the rice. Encourage her to find it using only her sense of touch. If very small children want to cheat and look with their eyes, that's okay, too.

Depending on your child's age or skill level, you can hide only one object at a time, just a few, or all of them at once.

For the slightly older child, hide a group of treasures in the rice. Tell her that you have hidden ten (or whatever number) objects and see if she can find them all. (Those magnetized alphabet letters that stick to the refrigerator work well for this game.)

Next, let your child hide objects for you to find!

VARIATIONS

♦ Rainbow Rice: If you want to make this game into a whole day's wonderful project, have your child help you color the rice different colors. You can do it one of two ways: Take a bowl of white rice, mix in some paint, and stir it until all the white rice is equally colored. Spread this mixture out on a newspaper and allow it to dry thoroughly. Make batches of several different colors.

Or, instead of using paints, use food coloring. (This is preferred if you have children who are likely to want to put the colorful rice in their mouths.)

Colored rice is captivating. I have yet to meet the child who doesn't want to play in it.

♦ Rice Rattles: You can turn the colorful rice into a musical instrument or a baby rattle by pouring it into two clear containers. Tape the containers together, their openings facing each other, using a strong tape, such as duct tape. The result is a shaker that makes a great sound.

I like to use clear film canisters for the baby rattle because it is just the right size for a baby's hands. Babies delight in watching the rice go from one end to the other.

For older children, plastic see-through cups work fine.

♦ Sand Treasures: If you have a sandbox, try this variation. Go around the house and gather things like erasers, large buttons, empty thread spools, film canisters, costume jewelry, pens, and so on to hide in the sand.

Count the number of things you have collected. Ask your child to close her eyes because you are going to bury (ten) secret things in the sandbox and she has to find them all.

WHAT IS BEING LEARNED

Children are learning how to "listen" with their fingers. The game requires them to be very quiet inside so they can "hear" what their fingers are telling them. Any time we can help our children learn to be calm and quietly focused, we are giving them a great gift.

Looking for something requires concentration and focusing, as we all know too well. If we get distracted, we can look in the same drawer many times and not see what we are looking for and then later find it in that very drawer. Giving a child this opportunity for success in finding hidden things increases her confidence as well as her ability to pay attention and stay focused in the moment. And no small gain for you is that you have someone who can use this skill to help you find where you last left your keys!

If you have played the variation where you have buried a certain number of objects and she has to find them all, she also gets experience in counting.

Envelope Shapes

Everything has its own shape, which can be determined by sight or by touch. In this game, children use both senses to identify common objects.

MATERIALS

common small household objects
envelopes
dark crayon

DIRECTIONS

Put a flat, textured object, such as a comb, in an envelope. Have your player try to guess what the object is by feeling it through the paper of the envelope. Then to see if he is right, or if he can't guess, have him do a rubbing. A rubbing is done by rubbing a dark crayon back and forth over the paper directly over the object until the shape seems to magically appear. Almost anything with a texture can be rubbed. (I've even seen rubbings of fish!)

Use different objects in different envelopes.

Idea possibilities:

◆ Things found around the house, such as a paper clip, different coins (dime, penny, quarter), a toothpick

◆ Things found in nature, such as a leaf or a piece of bark

You could talk about what shapes the objects have. For instance, the coin is a circle, the comb is more like a rectangle, and some leaves are like ovals.

VARIATION

◆ Mystery Bag: Use a tissue, handkerchief, sock, or anything similar as a bag and hide something small you have handy, such as a comb or lipstick, in it. Ask your child to feel the outside of the bag and guess what object is in it. Or put several objects in the bag and see if he can pull out the one you choose without looking.

This is a good way to pass the time when you're waiting somewhere, such as at the airport or doctor's office, using objects from your purse or pocket.

WHAT IS BEING LEARNED

Children are developing their sense of touch. When children are babies, they put everything in their mouths because it is their lips and tongue that are the most sensitive parts of their bodies. Later they learn that their fingertips can give them the same information without the risk of tasting something unpleasant. Feeling is a learned skill, and this game is one of the ways children can increase their sensitivity.

As children get older, they can get more and more sophisticated with their sense of touch. Help them increase their sensitivity by feeling the difference between a penny and a nickel or a toothpick and a small stick or different kinds of leaves.

Rubbing the shapes increases children's awareness of textures.

ALL AGES

One or two
people

Foot Writing

Playing this silly game helps develop the agility of children's feet, as well as their eye-foot coordination. It also gives the players (including you) a chance to do something they probably never did before.

MATERIALS

pencil or crayon
paper

DIRECTIONS

Have each player put a crayon or pencil between the big toe and the second toe of one foot and write letters on a piece of paper.

VARIATION

Draw pictures with your feet!

WHAT IS BEING LEARNED

Because this game takes a bit of practicing to get the desired results, it encourages concentration and focusing. It also helps train the foot to follow the directions of the eyes to develop better eye-foot coordination.

Footprint Game

This game takes a bit of preparation. But since the kids do the prep work, they're involved from moment one, which increases the scope of the things they learn along the way.

Two or more people

MATERIALS

paper
crayons or colored markers
Optional: clear Contac paper

DIRECTIONS

Give each child a piece of paper to stand on while she (or you or another child) outlines her foot (or both feet). Have the children make many footprints, sometimes outlining both feet on one piece of paper and sometimes outlining only one foot.

If they want to, players can color their foot outlines. Have some fun with this part by suggesting ways to make some unusual footprints, such as polka-dot feet, or a rainbow foot, or stripes, or whatever tickles their imagination. (If you want to use these foot patterns for more than one game, cover them with clear Contac paper or laminate them.)

Set out the course by laying the footprints out in a long line in singles or pairs.

How the players move from one piece of paper to the other depends on whether there are one or two footprints in front of them and how large the spaces are between the pieces of paper.

So if the first paper has two feet on it, the player jumps onto the paper with both feet. If the next one has only foot, the player hops onto it with either the right or left foot, depending on which foot was drawn (don't be too fussy about this distinction with younger children). If the footprint papers are laid down close together, it indicates small jumps or hops; if they are farther apart, it encourages long jumps or hops.

Let each player have a turn setting out the course for the others to follow and making up new rules, if wanted, such as "You have to jump and do a full circle in the air before you land whenever you get to rainbow feet."

VARIATIONS

Make outlines of hands, sometimes one hand, sometimes both hands, and lay them out with the footprints. When players go though the line, they may have to hop on one paper and then, while balancing on one foot, reach down and put two hands on the paper in front of them. Then they have to jump over that paper to the two footprints on the next paper.

Again, children can take turns laying out the papers so that they can directly affect the movements required.

Instead of using separate sheets of paper, you could also make a series of foot- and handprints on a long roll of butcher or shelf paper. Make more than one variation.

WHAT IS BEING LEARNED

Little ones learn how to outline their foot or another's foot on paper, which takes paying attention to the whole task and understanding the goal.

They also practice the hand-eye coordination task of "staying within the lines" (more or less) when coloring the foot.

All children get a chance to express their creativity by coloring the foot- or handprints in their own unique ways.

All children also get practice in jumping and hopping skills, which involve balance and strength.

And children get experience with following directions and the use of symbols; for example, a picture of one foot means to hop on that foot.

Older children get an opportunity to conceptualize and plan a course for others, taking into consideration factors such as how far the other kids can hop or jump, how many hops can be made in a row, how to incorporate the handprints into the movement, and so on.

Going Bats

Two or more people

I once did a workshop at a school for the deaf in Laos. I didn't speak a work of Laotian and none of the teachers spoke English so they couldn't translate my words into sign language. But by making simple bats out of rolled-up newspaper, we were able to play dozens of games without any communication except our body language. We started by having everyone get together in a circle. I threw my bat into the air and caught it. Soon everyone did the same, and then I threw it in a different way. Everyone did what I did. My helpers and some of the kids came up with other ways of throwing the bat, and everyone imitated them.

We had a great afternoon playing one game after another using these bats. Sometimes they were playing with such excitement that I made up the phrase "gross motor frenzy" to describe it.

We played the last game in a circle, softly blowing a feather from one person to the next, calming everyone.

As we were leaving, the children came outside and made a sign with their fingers that I knew well. It means "I love you."

Here are some of the other games that we played with the bats.

MATERIALS

newspaper

tape

DIRECTIONS

Roll up newspaper to form a bat and tape it closed. Try these different ways of tossing the bat and make up others.

♦ Hold the bat vertically and throw it from hand to hand.

♦ Toss it up in the air with the left hand and catch it with the right hand.

- Toss it up in the air with the right hand and catch it with the left hand.

- Toss the bat up and give it a half spin and catch the other end.

- Give it a spin so it twirls in a circle in the air before catching it.

- Drop it on your foot and kick it back up and catch it.

- Drop it on your knee and bounce it back up and catch it.

- Hold the bat horizontally and throw it up and catch it.

- Throw it up to increasingly higher distances. How high can it be thrown and still be caught?

- Balance it on your head, bend your head, and catch it.

- Bend your elbows at 90 degrees. Place the bat by your elbows and then straighten your arms. Catch the bat before it rolls off your arms.

VARIATIONS

- Jump the Bats: Lay the bats an equal distance apart as if they are the rungs of a paper ladder on the floor. Have the players start in front of the first bat and jump over each one.

   When the newness of the game begins to wear off, vary the distance between the bats so that the children have to vary the length of their jumps.

- Aim the Bats: Draw a target circle on a piece of paper and tape it to the wall. Or draw a circle on a chalkboard or dry-erase board that is already attached to the wall.

   Have the players stand a few feet back from the target circle, aim the bat as if it were a spear, and throw it at the target.

   Vary the distance the players stand from the target to increase or decrease the difficulty of the challenge.

   Play around with using different targets. If you are playing outside, the target could be an aluminum can on a fence post or an empty milk carton on a table or a hula hoop hanging from a tree branch. Let the children come up with their own ideas for targets.

- ♦ Bat Balance: Have players balance their bats vertically on their open palms. How long can the bats be kept upright? How long can they be kept upright while walking?

  Can bats be balanced on one finger? One foot? One knee? One elbow?

- ♦ Bat Reflex: Have players hold the bats vertically with one hand in front of them. Then they release the bats and see how quickly they can catch them with the other hand.

  Or have one player hold a bat vertically in front of another player at eye level. On the count of three, drop it. How quickly can the other player catch the bat?

  If you want, mark the spots on the bat where your players catch them each time. Try it a few times to see if the results improve with practice.

  Have players try each hand and see whether there is a difference between them.

- ♦ Bat Flexibility: Players start by holding the bats horizontally in front of their bodies, around thigh high. Then they bring the bats up and over their heads, behind their backs and legs, and finally step over them and end with the bats in the original starting position.

  Have players do this move a few times to maintain their flexibility.

- ♦ Bat Balance-Beam Walk: If you've played a lot of games with your newspaper bats and the bats are looking pretty wilted, you can get one more game out of them by laying them down end to end and asking your players to walk on them like a tightrope. Unlike a regular tightrope, however, you can make yours have all sorts of angles, which encourages children to watch where their feet are going!

WHAT IS BEING LEARNED

Each game has its own special kinesthetic learning experience: eye-hand coordination, eye-foot coordination, strength, balance, flexibility, and, oh yes—how to have a good time with a rolled-up newspaper.

Gentle Ball Games

There are lots of ways to play ball games that don't involve a hard ball coming at you at a fast pace, and there are many kinds of kinder, gentler balls, as well.

I was never big on games like Dodge 'Em, where children had to get out of the way of a hard ball that was being thrown at them. I'd feel the sting of a ball that bounced off my body and I'd think, "Why is this fun again?"

What I like best about these game is that everyone, regardless of age or skill level, can play them together. Each player becomes involved with the individual task of throwing her own ball, and that takes so much focus that most players won't bother comparing their skills with those of others. Everyone is trying for her personal best, and that personal best keeps growing with each practice.

MATERIALS

"gentle balls": either homemade out of plastic bags or newspaper or beans in a sock, or store-bought beach balls, foam balls, beanbags, scarves, or pillows

DIRECTIONS

Make gentle balls or, best of all, have the players make their own.

◆ Newspaper Balls: Scrunch up one or two pages of newspaper into a ball shape and put some tape or cloth around it to keep that shape. The more pages used, the bigger the ball.

◆ Plastic Bag Ball: Put a few plastic bags into one bag and twist it closed. Tie it tight using the handles of the bag. (There's no way to do this one wrong; just tie it any way you can to keep it closed and in a ball shape.)

◆ Beanbags: Throw some dried beans into the toe of a sock and make a knot in the top of the sock.

Standing on
One Foot

If you use store-bought balls instead, here are some things to consider.

- ◆ Beach balls are great for younger children because they are large, lightweight, and easier to catch than small balls.

- ◆ Foam balls and balls such as Koosh balls are good for grasping. If they have dangly things hanging from them, children get more things to grasp at.

- ◆ Beanbags are great because they feel good and never roll away.

- ◆ Scarves, which can be used in throwing games, too, fall so gently when they are tossed in the air that the catcher has a longer time to make the catch.

- ◆ Pillows, scarves, and rag dolls are all easy to grasp and make it easier to learn how to catch with one hand.

Catching with Nondominant Hand

Clapping before Catching

After everyone has a ball, call out these instructions and give the players time to try out each idea.

- ◆ Throw low and catch with two hands.
- ◆ Throw higher and higher, catching with two hands.
- ◆ Throw the ball up and clap one time before you catch it. Clap twice. Clap three times.
- ◆ Put the ball on your head. Bend your head forward and catch it.
- ◆ Catch the ball while standing on one foot.
- ◆ Start low and catch with one hand, your dominant hand.
- ◆ Catch with your nondominant hand, putting your preferred hand in your pocket or behind your body.
- ◆ Catch the ball underhand by letting it fall into a cupped hand.

- ◆ Catch the ball overhand by grabbing the falling ball out of the air.
- ◆ Put the ball on the backs of your hands. Toss it up and catch it.
- ◆ Catch the ball with one eye closed. Catch it with both eyes closed!
- ◆ Throw the ball up high, turn around in a circle, and catch it.
- ◆ Lie down and throw the ball, then stand up to catch it.
- ◆ Walk and keep the ball in the air by bouncing it off the backs of your hands.
- ◆ How far can you throw the ball? Can you throw it farther the next time?

WHAT IS BEING LEARNED

These games give children another opportunity to practice eye-hand coordination. Watch a very young child throw her first ball and you'll see her eyes looking one way and her hands throwing another. She doesn't yet know that it's her eyes that direct her hands and that "watching what you are doing" really does makes a difference. Learning eye-hand coordination paves the way for such later skills as writing words, putting the tiniest tile into an intricate mosaic, or measuring the exact ingredients for a complicated sauce.

When we are directing with our minds and watching with our eyes, we can accomplish anything we want with our hands.

Do Your Own Thing

Two or more people

Here's an opportunity for children to show off their creative selves using movement. You can make up your own ways for your children to move or use some of the ideas below. Either way, it's fun for everyone.

MATERIALS

pieces of paper or newspaper

DIRECTIONS

Put some pieces of paper or newspaper on the floor and start by asking ask each child to go from piece to piece using the method of locomotion you call out. You can vary the request depending on the age or coordination skills of your players. Next, let the players make up moves for the others to do.

Possibilities, listed from easy to hard:

♦ March from one paper to another.

♦ Walk on tiptoes from paper to paper.

♦ Jump and clap hands with each jump.

♦ Jump sideways with hands on hips.

♦ Jump backward with hands on knees.

♦ Jump forward two and jump back one.

♦ Jump from paper to paper with closed eyes.

♦ Land on each paper in a squat position.

♦ Hop while patting head and rubbing belly.

♦ Jump and twirl in a full circle in the air with each jump.

♦ Do a karate kick with each jump.

WHAT IS BEING LEARNED

When playing Do Your Own Thing, children get experience with a variety of movements and get to use their creativity to make up their own movement ideas. When they are imitating each other's movements, they need to notice how the others are moving (what are the legs doing, what is the position of the arms, what is the facial expression) and internally figure out how to mimic that movement.

Leap, Run, and Slalom

This game is like Do Your Own Thing in that it uses that wonderfully ubiquitous material, newspaper.

You can also use recycled photocopy paper or even used envelopes. Feel free to modify the materials with whatever is handy and fits the motor skills of your players.

MATERIALS

any kind of paper

DIRECTIONS

Lay one piece of paper down and call it "home base." Explain that each player starts from there. Then lay another piece down in front of home base. Each player leaps over that piece, starting from home base.

Keep adding pieces of paper, one at a time, until the player needs to jump over them all!

The challenge in this game is progressive. I find that kids get excited and want me to put all the papers down right away so they can immediately leap over them all! But it's best to do it a piece at a time so they can feel the difference between using all their strength when leaping and using just a little.

There are two ways to do the leaping. One is for the players to take a running start. This would mean that you would put the sections farther from home base. The other way is for players to jump from a standing position. In this case the sections should be placed directly in front of home base.

Try both ways.

VARIATIONS

◆ Slalom Run: Lay pieces of paper out in a line, each one about 12 inches from the other. The children run from the first to the last by weaving in and out between the sections like a slalom skier. The object is to see how fast they can go without touching the sections.

Other ways to play are:

◇ Bounce a ball while weaving between the sections.

◇ Kick a newspaper ball around the sections.

◇ Have two children go together, the one behind holding the waist of the one in front. (This is a good technique to use for the child who doesn't know how to slalom run and can learn by holding on to someone who does).

◆ Choo-Choo Slalom: Have several players line up to form a train, which weaves in and out between the sections. The engine of the train has to be sure she leaves enough room for the rest of the train, especially the caboose, to make it around the sections without touching them.

WHAT IS BEING LEARNED

When playing the leaping game, children are learning about modifying their force. This is especially good for kids who don't know how to "pull their punches" and sometimes hit harder than they meant to.

When playing the slalom game, children are learning to internally plan their movements so they can keep changing directions as needed. Physical and occupational therapists call this ability "motor planning," and children who keep bumping into people and things need work on this skill.

Two or more people

Jumping Joys

Kids love to jump. Besides the instant joy of defying gravity and being airborne, there's a technical reason. When we jump, or, more precisely, when we land from a jump, our whole propioceptive system is stimulated. Since this is the system that sends information from our joints and muscles to our brain, jumping sends the message: "We are all here now!" After I play a jumping game during morning circle at preschools, children are much more alert and present.

This game is about jumping over a rope that keeps getting progressively higher and then going under a rope that gets progressively lower. In the thirty-five years I've played with children all over the world, I must have done this game thousands of times. It's always a sure winner.

MATERIALS

rope, string, or long scarf
Optional: paper or tape

DIRECTIONS

You can play this game with one child or with a group.

Tie one end of a piece of rope or string or a long scarf to something solid and hold the other end. Or use two people, each holding an end.

Start with the rope down low. Ask your players to get a running start and jump over the rope, one at a time. (You might want to mark the starting spot with a piece of paper or tape.) Then raise the rope a smidgen and

ask them to do it again from the same side. Keep making the rope progressively higher until it is too high for anyone to jump over.

Children sometimes get so excited with this game that they want to turn right around and jump again and could end up bumping into the person running from the correct direction. Rather than tell them what *not* to do, give them rules. Either tell them when they've finished jumping to go around the person holding the rope and back to the start or wait until everyone is on the same side. (Remember to give the person holding the rope a turn or use that job as a way of including someone who is unable to jump.)

Needless to say, if it looks as if a player is not going to make it over the rope, lower the rope.

After the players have all jumped as high as they can, have them go under the rope, limbo-style, if they want, until everyone has had a turn. Start with the rope up high, then keep lowering it until the players have to crawl on their bellies to get under it without touching it.

Sometimes it's fun to pantomime that the rope is hot (zzzzz!) and they better be careful not to touch it! Children enjoy this kind of dangerless danger.

VARIATIONS

♦ Use two ropes so that the players have to jump twice—once over each rope. Vary the height of each rope so that the players have to jump high over one and jump low over another, or jump over one and go under the other.

♦ Hold two ropes level but apart so that the player has to jump over a wider area. Call it a creek. Move the strings farther apart and call it a river that the children have to jump over without falling in and getting wet! Want to try for an ocean? Or put some pieces of paper in the middle and call them stepping-stones and have the children leap from one to the other and then over the rope.

♦ Use three ropes and let your inventiveness be your guide!

WHAT IS BEING LEARNED

Children are learning how to modify their energy to accomplish a goal. It takes more energy to jump over a higher rope than a lower one.

They are also learning how to control their energy. If they have to jump over one rope and then crawl under the next one, they have to halt their momentum and change it to fit the next task. In the therapy trade, we call that motor control.

They also have to plan their movements. If they are to go under a rope that is lower than it was previously, they have to organize their movements so that they are closer to the ground. The official name for this is motor planning.

Whether they are modifying, controlling, or planning, this game helps children learn even more about moving through space and making their bodies do whatever they want.

Ballooning Inside

Playing with balloons can be magical, like playing with air wrapped in color. Bring out a balloon and everyone—children and adults alike—can't help but light up a little. Here are a variety of ways of playing with a balloon.

Two or more people

MATERIALS

balloon

DIRECTIONS

Start with the old traditional how-many-times-can-the-players-hit-the-balloon-and-keep-it-up-in-the-air-before-it-touches-the-ground game. Any number of players can play together to cooperatively keep the ball up in the air.

Every time the balloon touches the ground, start from number 1 again. What's the highest number you can reach?

VARIATIONS

Use different body parts to hit the balloon. For example, bat the balloon with only your head, or elbow, or one finger.

Play balloon volleyball by stringing a piece of rope between a stable object on one side of the room and a stable object on the other side. The height of the rope depends on the size of your players. Form teams with one team on each side of the rope, and bat the balloon back and forth over the rope.

Keep the rules really loose. If little ones hit the balloon under the rope to the other side or even run with it to the other side, that counts. The only rule is to have as much fun as possible!

WHAT IS BEING LEARNED

Children learn eye-hand coordination and teamwork, and everyone learns that playing together can often be more fun than watching television.

Instant Relay

Group activity

A quick and easy relay game can be played with pieces of newspaper or any type of paper.

One thing is standard in a relay game: It goes from Point A to Point B and then returns to Point A.

How one gets from Point A to Point B is up for grabs.

MATERIALS

paper

DIRECTIONS

Put one piece of paper down to mark Point A, the starting point, and another to mark Point B, the goal.

Each team of three should have its own set of markers so that no player has to wait too long for a turn.

How close or far apart Points A and B are depends on the skill and energy of your group or your mood. You might want the kids to run a long way to get them physically ready to do something quiet next. You might want to make it shorter so that they concentrate more on the quality of their movements and not on speed or endurance. It's all good.

This could be a competition or each team could get points if everyone on the team finishes—somewhere between fifty and a zillion points and everyone wins.

Here are some possibilities for the relay. The players could also take turns making up their own set of fun rules:

♦ Each player runs from Point A to Point B, hops around Point B, and runs back to Point A to tag the next player on the team.

♦ Each player walks backward from Point A to Point B, skips around Point B backward, and runs back to Point A to tag the next player on the team.

♦ Each player skips from Point A to Point B, jumps over Point B, and hops back to Point A to tag the next player on the team.

♦ Each player gallops from Point A to Point B, stands on Point B and sings out his name, then marches back to Point A to tag the next player on the team.

♦ Each player "bear walks" from Point A to Point B (a bear walk is like a crawl, except that you extend your legs and walk on flat feet), stands on Point B while touching his nose to his toes, and twirls back to Point A to tag the next player on the team.

And so on!

If you'd like to use a relay baton, you could easily make one out of rolled-up newspaper.

WHAT IS BEING LEARNED

Moving in a variety of movement patterns enlarges one's internal motor

vocabulary. The more ways one learns to move one's body, the more awareness is acquired.

Children also get to strengthen their memory skills by remembering
the rules: What comes first? What happens when I stand on the square?
How am I supposed to move to get back? This is a great practice for a life-
time of needing to remember sequences. ("First I'll stop at the store, then
the bank, then turn in the proposal, then . . .")

Wiggly Snake

Two or more
people

*If your children are too young to jump rope or if your rope jumpers are
looking for a new game, try Wiggly Snake. I always find that the
challenge entices children to play it.*

MATERIALS

rope

DIRECTIONS

Holding one end of a rope, let the other
end trail enticingly on the floor. Gently
shake your end so that the rope wiggles as it
moves. As you walk around, ask your child if
she can step on the wiggly snake and make it stop.

How quickly or slowly you move the rope away from the
stomping foot is your call. You have the ability to make the
game wonderfully challenging or annoyingly frustrating or stupidly
easy. You can always start easy, until both you and the players get the sense
of the game, and then up the challenge.

VARIATION

If you have more than one player, have each player take a turn controlling the rope. Each person's unique style will affect the game. Remind the rope holder that the rope must stay in contact with the ground. No one can step on a rope in the air!

WHAT IS BEING LEARNED

Children are learning about eye-foot coordination and about balancing. They are also improving their reflexes, because they have only a milli-second to stomp on the rope before it moves on.

Tube Sock Throw

I like this game because it takes two seconds to make the ball. Children can just play around with it or they can practice and get really accurate at hitting targets with it.

Two or more people

MATERIALS

3 or 4 tube socks or knee socks

DIRECTIONS

To make the ball, roll up a couple of socks and tuck them into the toe of a tube sock or knee sock. Players hold the top of the sock, swing the ball around their heads, then let go and see how far it goes.

Players can throw the ball to each other or throw it alone and measure the distance thrown each time.

They can also aim at a target and learn how to really direct a tube sock!

WHAT IS BEING LEARNED

In addition to eye-hand coordination that children learn from any throwing and aiming game, they learn how much force in needed to throw a farther distance.

Target Ball

You know the little thrill you get when your crumpled piece of paper goes in the wastebasket on the other side of the room? These games provide the same little thrill of success.

When my youngest child was two years old, she toddled over to me with her empty yogurt container and a walnut and suggested we play a target game with them. I knew this kindred spirit had gotten the message on the fun of aiming for a target.

MATERIALS

> paper or tape
> common objects found around the house
> easy things to throw, such as foam balls, beanbags, walnuts, acorns, or
>   Ping-Pong balls

DIRECTIONS

Place a piece of paper or tape on the floor to mark the spot from which the player throws. The player can sit or stand on the marker. Lay down a variety of targets at varying distances from the marker. Place some targets close to the player so that they are very easy to hit and others at progressively more challenging distances away. Use some targets that have wide openings and others that are smaller.

If there is more than one player, put down more markers so the players can throw at the same time if they want to.

You can give a point score to each target, but make the scoring humorous to avoid excessive competition between two or more players. For example, the wastebasket could be worth a zillion two points and the dishpan a gazillion points!

Here are some suggestions for targets:

wastebasket

dishpan

bucket

boxes

coffee can

shoes

upside-down chairs

rope coil

hula hoop

VARIATIONS

Target games are great to play outside with things that are easy to find, such as an inner tube, a bicycle tire, a coiled garden hose, street signs, a hole in the ground, big rocks, and telephone poles.

WHAT IS BEING LEARNED

Children learn the eye-hand coordination lesson of making the ball go where they want it to.

They are also learning that a target game can be made out of anything, and they are getting practice for that big moment when they slam-dunk a crumpled ball of paper into the wastebasket across the room.

Hold Tight/Let Go

Two or more
people

Feeling the difference between being tense and being relaxed is not always as obvious as you might think. Sometimes our shoulders can be up by our ears and we may not be aware of it until someone points it out.

This physical awareness of how we are holding our bodies can be developed by experiencing consciously what a relaxed body feels like, muscle by muscle.

DIRECTIONS

Say the following instructions to your players, or record them onto a tape and play it back so that you can join in the activity.

"Lie down on your back and close your eyes. Just lie there for a moment. You don't have to do anything or go anywhere. This is a quiet moment for you just to lie there and do nothing."

Pause.

"Now I want you to scrunch up your forehead like you are very worried. Make your forehead very wrinkled. Scrunch it up tight, tighter, tighter . . . now let it go. Let it totally go so that it feels like water spreading out."

Pause.

"Now scrunch up your whole face, press your lips together, suck in your cheeks, squint your eyes, wrinkle your forehead. Make your face tight, tighter, tighter . . . and now let it go. Let it completely relax so your cheeks feel loose and your eyelids feel droopy and your face is totally relaxed."

Pause.

"Now bring your shoulders up toward your ears. Make them very, very tense. Pull them up tight, tighter, and even tighter . . . now let them drop. Completely let go of them and let them fall back into the floor so you have no control of them at all. Let them just lie there, completely relaxed."

Pause.

"Now tense your arms. Make energy shoot from your shoulder, down your arms, and out your hands. Your arms are so stiff that they don't even touch the floor anymore. Tense them more, more, more . . . and now let them go. Completely let all tension out of your arms so they are lying on the floor and feeling like they are melting through the floor, completely relaxed."

Pause.

"Tense your chest and back. Feel like you are turning into a robot and your back and chest are getting stiffer and stiffer and stiffer. Now let it go and just let your body fall into the floor, completely letting go of your spine."

Pause.

"Now tighten up your legs and feet—both legs, both feet. Point your toes hard, harder. Make your legs and feet so tense and tight that they no longer touch the floor—tight , tighter, tighter. Now let them go. Let them go completely so you feel they are melting into the floor, completely and totally relaxed.

"Just lie there and feel a wave of relaxation wash over you so your body feels heavy and almost separate from you. Let your body completely melt into the floor while you do nothing except watch your breath go in . . . and out . . . and in . . . and out. For the next few moments, do nothing but watch your breath, letting your body completely relax."

WHAT IS BEING LEARNED

Children are learning to be aware of how they are feeling by noticing the difference between a contracted muscle and a relaxed muscle. This inner awareness will help them know when they are feeling stressed, and this game will give them a method for releasing that tension.

Eyedropper Art

I often bring an eyedropper and a jar of water in my bag of tricks when I'm working with a child on fine motor control. I find that children are fascinated with the challenge of putting a small tube in water and making it fill up. Their ability to copy my example, follow my instructions, or figure it out on their own also gives me a sense of their cognitive development.

Recently, on a hot day, a child and I discovered that we could fill up our eyedroppers with water and squirt them at each other! Talk about fun!

Two or more people

MATERIALS

eyedropper
paint or food coloring in water
paper

DIRECTIONS

Using an eyedropper filled with paint or colored water, try these art projects:

- ◆ Drop some paint from just above the paper. Keep dropping paint from higher and higher distances, and notice the difference in the results.

- ◆ Drop a few drops of different colors of paint on the paper, then fold the paper in half. Open the paper to see a symmetrical design.

- ◆ Drop a big drop of one color of paint on the paper and then speckle it with little drops of another color.

- ◆ Drop paint on different surfaces, such as dry, wet, or damp paper or wax paper or aluminum foil. How are the results different?

- ◆ Drop puddles of paint on the paper and then tip the paper in various ways to make the paint run.

VARIATIONS

There's no end to the possibilities for thing to paint with. Try sponges, cotton balls, powder puffs, toothbrushes, shoe brushes, cotton swabs, and corks. Or just put a blob of paint on a piece of paper and blow at it with a straw!

Instead of just painting on paper, try painting on burlap, wood, cardboard, grocery bags, and rocks.

WHAT IS BEING LEARNED

This is a fine motor and cognitive activity that encourages creativity. Children, using their finger muscles, learn how and when to squeeze the eyedropper bulb in order to fill it up and empty it so that they can create art.

Toothpick Sculptures

*A box of raisins and a handful of toothpicks can keep children entertained
for a long while and bring out their creativity. Bring some in a plastic bag
on the next airplane ride or lay the raisins out on the kitchen table and
make sculptures together. If all that happens is that your child wants to
spear the raisins and eat them, that's worthwhile, too. Raisins provide a
good source for the daily iron requirement.*

MATERIALS

   toothpicks
   raisins

DIRECTIONS

Combine cut-up or whole toothpicks and
raisins to make abstract sculptures or
models of animals, people, or buildings
(see illustration).

VARIATION

You can use softened dried peas or mini-
marshmallows instead of raisins.

WHAT IS BEING
LEARNED

Young children are getting a
chance to practice coordinating the small muscles of their
hands.

   All children are getting
another opportunity to develop
their creativity. They are learning

how to take an idea and manifest it. With these simple materials, the time between the thought and the manifestation is satisfyingly quick.

Stone Painting

My Australian friend Jane, who homeschools her four children, showed me this nifty little trick of painting on rocks using water instead of paint. It makes whatever you write look like calligraphy. If you don't like what you did, your "mistake" dries up and vanishes, but in reality everything you paint this way looks good!

MATERIALS

   paintbrush
   water
   dark flat rock

DIRECTIONS

Have children dip the paintbrush in the water and try out different designs on the rock. Let them use their imagination to draw whatever they want.

VARIATIONS

This is a good way for little ones to practice writing their numbers or letters.

   Older children could take turns making designs that you or others try to copy.

WHAT IS BEING LEARNED

This activity exercises the small muscles of the hand and the large muscle of imagination. Children can feel free to try out any design because whatever is created is for that moment and then disappears. It is a lot less intimidating than paper.

Using the variation of having children make letters and numbers gives them a safe place to experiment with writing.

Using the variation of copying each other's designs gives the players an opportunity to notice details and direction.

Penny Flick

You're sitting in a restaurant waiting for the food to come and you can feel the children are starting to get restless. Stop the disruption before it even starts with a captivating and quiet game of Penny Flick. It's a game with many variations, so you can keep introducing new ways to keep the children happy and busy right up until the food comes!

Or play this game at home after everyone's finished eating, the dishes are off the table, and you want to prolong and savor the family moment.

I've also successfully played this game with small groups of senior citizens. No one, it seems, can resist a chance to flick a penny.

MATERIALS

pennies

DIRECTIONS

Give all the players a penny and show them how to move the penny along the table by flicking their index finger and thumb or pushing it with just their index finger or the side of their thumb. They can use whatever finger method works best for them. The method doesn't matter. Introduce one or more of the games below or make up your own:

♦ All the players flick their pennies into the center of the table and try to get the pennies to bump into each other.

♦ Players sitting across from each other flick their pennies toward each other, trying to get them to touch.

♦ Two objects, such as the salt and pepper shaker or just two other pennies, are set up a short distance away from the flickers as "goal posts." The players have to flick their pennies between the two objects. Keep making the goal posts closer together to increase the challenge.

♦ Using a straw or spoon handle as a hockey stick, call the penny a "puck" and bat the puck back and forth between the players.

♦ Make a line of pennies and have the players try to hit each penny and knock it out of line.

♦ Make a line of pennies with at least an inch of space between them, and have the player try to flick her penny through each of the spaces. Make the first space the largest and each following space progressively smaller.

♦ Place a penny on its edge, give it a little push, and watch it roll. See how far it can go without falling over.

♦ Try rolling a penny with each hand at the same time.

VARIATION

Instead of pennies, scrunch up a tiny piece of napkin or newspaper into a ball shape. Bottle caps also work well.

WHAT IS BEING LEARNED

The small muscles of the hand are getting a workout in this game, along with the awareness of how to assess the energy output of those muscles to produce the desired results.

PART FIVE

Games That Enhance Interpersonal Skills

Interpersonal skills are the ability to interact with others, understand them, interpret their behavior, and feel comfortable in their company. As social animals, we tend to thrive and grow when involved with others and need these skills to exist socially. Children who are strong in interpersonal skills seek out the company of others and are easily able to interpret others' body language, facial expressions, and tone of voice, and to respond accordingly.

The games in this section are ways for you and your child to play together and with others. Children need easy, no-stress, hang-out time as a way to connect with their social selves. The group games are cooperative, where the social action is cheering for each other, having a common goal, or moving in sync. All the games show children the delightful side of being social.

AGES 6 AND UNDER

Two or more
people

Who's in the Box?

A large box arrives in your life. Maybe your new computer was inside, or a large printer. Do you throw it away? Hold everything! If you have a crawler, toddler, or young preschooler, first it's time to play Who's in the Box?

MATERIALS

large box

DIRECTIONS

Set the box on its end so that the front flaps open like a pair of French doors. Ask your snookems to go inside the box and close the flaps.

Then knock politely on the flap and say, "Who's in the box?"

At this point he will probably push open the flaps and show his smiling, giggling face, and you, of course, will say with great surprise, "Why, it's (child's name)!"

Don't be surprised if your young player wants to go inside the box and do it again—and again—and again—and again . . .

VARIATION

A version of this game can be played in a school setting. It's a fun and unusual addition to the usual morning circle games.

Place the box in the front of the class. Ask the players to put their heads down to cover their eyes or turn their backs to the box. Then, when their eyes are covered or their backs are turned, pick up one child, put him into the box, and close the flap.

Tell the children they can look now. Have the children look around and notice who is missing, then guess who is in the box.

To also work on timing and rhythm, I have them chant before they announce their guess:

"Knock knock, who's in the box?

It's _____!"

Then we all clap and shout as that child emerges from the box.

WHAT IS BEING LEARNED

This game is really a bigger version of Peekaboo, the perennial favorite. As you've no doubt found in any child development book, this type of game is a way for children to learn the idea that people and objects still exist even when they can't be seen.

A baby who panics when Mom gets out of the car to come around and open the door doesn't know this yet. As little ones begin to get this concept, it is easier for them to be left at day care or at home when you leave for work. They know you still exist somewhere else and they'll see you again. Peekaboo!

Children who are past the Peekaboo stage still like to go inside a box and have their own little world where they don't have to say "boo" to anyone!

In the school setting, children are expanding their social awareness beyond themselves and a few others to noticing everyone who is in their class that day, as well as everyone who is missing.

They also get to have the thrill of feeling noticed when they pop out of the box and everyone enthusiastically applauds.

A Stone's Throw

One or two people

If you like to take a walk with your child and go off the main road to sit beside a creek, you'll like playing A Stone's Throw. This throwing game will give her a delightful experience in playing with another.

I was playing this game one day with a four-year-old child with Down syndrome. To take the sting away from possible misses (my aim is not that great, either), I began saying "Got one!" and "Missed one!" with the same enthusiasm. I found him quick to imitate my tone, and I noticed we would giggle just as much at the misses as at the successes.

MATERIALS

pebbles

DIRECTIONS

Gather up a pile of pebbles and then take turns throwing them at a nearby rock. If you're not at a creek, it doesn't matter; this game can be played in town by throwing pebbles at a lamppost, a fence picket, or even a wall.

To make the game more even, the person with the weaker or less accurate throw can sit closer to the target. (Don't feel bad if that person is you.)

Pick different targets to aim at or see how many you can hit with your eyes closed.

WHAT IS BEING LEARNED

Some children are loners by choice. Some children tend to play by themselves because they haven't had much experience in playing with others. As busy parents, we can still help our children discover the rewards of playing with others by taking a walk and playing a friendly game like A Stone's Throw.

One or two
people

Poker-Chip Play

Putting things into other things is a baby's idea of a good time. They delight in taking everything out, such as all the toys in the toy basket, and later in their development, they delight in putting everything back in (we hope, anyway).

This game feeds that desire to empty things and adds an extra challenge to the putting things back, which makes it even more interesting.

A surprising thing about this activity is that although it is meant for the toddler, I have found that many children even as old as ten relish playing this game. I think it's something about the satisfaction of putting things neatly away and getting it all done. Perhaps it is also about feeling in control of things that disappear.

MATERIALS

clean plastic container with lid
poker chips

DIRECTIONS

Take an empty yogurt, cottage cheese, or similar type of container with a lid and cut a slot in the top that is slightly bigger than a poker chip.

Place ten or so poker chips inside the container and put the slotted top back on. Let your baby shake the container and delight in the interesting noise it makes.

Then help him take the top off and discover the treasure inside! After he has had time to explore the chips, which might involve tasting, throwing, and tossing, show him how to put the chips through the slot and back into the container. It's a skill he'll use later when he is putting his pennies into his piggy bank.

WHAT IS BEING LEARNED

On the cognitive level, baby is learning about "object permanence," the understanding that things don't disappear when you don't see them but are somewhere else. This game, where chips disappear into a slot and then reappear when the top is removed, is a very reassuring lesson.

Babies also learn how to maneuver an object to fit into a specified space. If you turn the container so that sometimes the slot is horizontal to your learner and sometimes vertical, he learns how he has to maneuver his wrist to make the poker chip match up.

A People Sandwich

This game is guaranteed to bring giggles. It's all about making a sandwich using some children as the ingredients. The other children then get to pretend they are "eating" that delicious sandwich. Yum.

DIRECTIONS

Have the children stand in a circle. Announce that you are going to make a sandwich, and pick one child to stand in the center of the circle and be the bread. Then ask, "What else shall we put in this sandwich?" If at first the children don't come up with ideas, suggest some: "Let's add some cheese." Then pick another child to be the cheese and put her directly in front of the child who is the bread. Continue with the ingredients, such as ham, pickles, tomato, lettuce, and so on, and end with another piece of bread. Each time, place the child in front of the last ingredient. You can be the one who picks the child who will be each ingredient, but you'll probably find that they are jumping up and down excitedly to be the next piece. You might also find, like I did, that a child might call out an ingredient that isn't usually in a sandwich, such as rice. Go ahead and put some rice in the sandwich!

After the sandwich is made, everyone pretends to eat it, smacking their lips and making chewing sounds. (This is what brings the giggles.)

Then start all over and make a new sandwich!

WHAT IS BEING LEARNED

Children are experimenting with a fun way to play with each other. Playing pretend is an important skill. Everyone pretending together reinforces their sense of being part of the group.

Of course, there is also the culinary lesson of what goes into a good sandwich!

The Same Inside

A new child was joining the Head Start school and his mother was very worried. Her four-year-old son couldn't speak or hear or walk, but he had feelings, and his mother was afraid that the children would find him too odd to understand and befriend. She asked the Special Ed teacher, his aide, and me to come up with some way to introduce him to the group.

We did a puppet show. Our puppets were simple—just happy children's faces taped onto Popsicle sticks, but one of the smiling faces was inside a paper wheelchair. The puppet children in the play's script asked all sorts of questions. In the end they realized that although Nathan wasn't the same as them on the outside and did many things differently, inside he was just like them.

MATERIALS

easily made puppets

DIRECTIONS

Have the children make simple puppets to represent themselves out of easy-to-find materials. For example, tape faces to Popsicle sticks or draw faces on the fingers of a work glove.

If you want to make one puppet have a physical challenge, make an appropriate addition: sunglasses for a blind child, little button in the ear of a deaf child, chair with paper wheels for the child who uses a wheelchair, and so on.

You could make the play be about the children playing a game, such as Duck Duck Goose, and then have them wonder aloud why this one child is not playing. Have them ask the child questions.

Here are some examples of the ones we used:

One puppet: Why don't you get up and run?

Nathan puppet (played by Nathan's aide): Because my legs are not strong enough yet.

Another puppet friend: Why do you sit in a chair?

Nathan puppet: Because it is easier to move around with wheels.

Another puppet friend: Can you talk?

Nathan puppet: I can't talk yet, but I can show you how I feel. Watch me. Say "Hi" to me.

(The whole group said "Hi" and we turned the puppet face around so that an even bigger smile face showed.)

Puppet friend: Do you like to play?

Nathan puppet: Oh yes, just like you.

Puppet friend: Do you like toys?

Nathan puppet: Oh yes, just like you.

Puppet friend: Do you love your mommy?

Nathan puppet: Oh yes, just like you.

Then we sang this song to reflect the play's theme (to the tune of the *Beverly Hillbillies* theme):

We're different on the outside but the same inside.
Some of us are skinny
And some of us are wide,
Some of us are tall
And some of us are small,
And as we knows
We all wear different clothes.

We're just different on the outside,
We're the same inside.
Some days we've been happy
And some days we've cried,

Some days we feel silly
And sometimes we get mad.
And that's because we're just the same inside.

We're different on the outside, but the same in the end.
We all love our mothers
And we all love our friends.
We all love the ocean and the trees and the sand.
And that's because we're all the same inside.

We're different on the outside, but the same inside,
A little different on the outside and the same inside.
Our hearts are the same
But not our hides.
But it's okay, we're all the same inside.

WHAT IS BEING LEARNED

Accepting diversity seems to be the challenge of this century. In order to have lasting peace and love, we are going to have to accept each other and ourselves just as we are. Children with special needs often provide other children with their first chance to meet someone who is different and yet, they soon find out, a lot like them. They like to play. They like to laugh. They want to have fun, too. We want children to learn that we are different on the outside, and isn't that interesting? We are the same inside, and isn't that nice?

Lily Pads

This game is a fun no-loser version of Musical Chairs with many possible variations and opportunities for kids to interact.

Group activity

MATERIALS

newspaper

DIRECTIONS

Lay down newspaper sections on the floor so each child has his own.
Explain to the group that these are not really newspapers, they are lily pads,
and that they aren't really kids, they are frogs. (Of course—what else?)
Have each frog stand on a lily pad while you put on music or sing a song.
While the music is happening, the frogs have to jump around, froglike,
until the music stops, at which point they have to madly race to any pad.
You will have, of course, removed one pad. But in this game the padless
player isn't out. Instead she has to share a pad with another frog. When
the music, or your singing, starts up again, you can suggest different ways
they must move each time—skipping, walking backward, hopping, and
so on. As you take more and more pads away, the remaining pads will get
very crowded. So that everyone can fit, the rule is that some part of each
frog's body has to touch the pad.

VARIATION

Instead of lily pads, you can go back to Musical Chairs, but change the rules to make it into a no-loser version: remove the chairs, not the people. Play as you would normally by removing the chairs, but no one is out. At the end there will be a big pile-up on one chair. (You can warn everyone ahead of time that at the end there will be a pile of people so that those who don't want to get squished can opt out.)

WHAT IS BEING LEARNED

This game encourages physical closeness, which has a way of making kids feel friendlier toward one another. Most people enjoy physical touch, but group situations are not commonly set up for this to occur. Young boys tend to meet this need by wrestling with their peers. Girls often hug.

In the Lily Pad game, children get the opportunity to be physically close and also to help each other. Success in this game is working together to get everyone on the last pad so they all can win.

AGES 6 AND UP

Stepping on Tails

This high-energy group game is good for burning off excess sugar energy after birthday party treats. In the classroom, it's a good activity to precede quiet sit-down tasks.

Group activity

MATERIALS

    scissors
    ball of string

DIRECTIONS

Cut a piece of string for each player that is long enough to hang, dragging along the ground, when tucked into a waistband.

The object of the game is for the children to run after each other and try to step on each other's dragging strings, causing the strings to fall out. Children try to collect as many "tails" as they can while still keeping their own.

Children can also work in pairs in which they agree to go after certain players together and to protect each other's backs from attack.

No one is ever "out" of the game. Even if a child's string is stepped on and caught, he can still go after others. However, the one with the most strings can be declared "The One with the Most Strings." This title avoids that winner/loser mentality while accurately stating what happened.

(If a child is wearing a dress, first tie one string around her waist and tuck the hanging string into that.)

VARIATIONS

- Instead of string, you could use crepe paper streamers or ribbons.
- Children could grab the string (or crepe paper or ribbon) with their hands instead of stepping on it with their feet.

WHAT IS BEING LEARNED

Socially, children are learning to be aware of each other as they look for who lost their string and who still has a string to step on. When playing in pairs, they have a sense of connection with each other and a responsibility to watch out for each other.

Children are also learning to improve their agility and eye-foot coordination. Like eye-hand coordination, eye-foot coordination teaches children that their eyes direct where their foot goes. Children who trip over obstacles in their path are still working on that awareness.

The game also reinforces spatial awareness by being aware of what is happening in all directions. Children need to not only focus on stepping on another string, they also have to be aware of who is coming and in what direction for their string.

Push Me/Pull You

This is a game that speaks to females, I've noticed. It's a game in which you get to pit all your physical strength against another. We women don't get many opportunities to do that. We lift weights; we carry heavy boxes; we pick up children. But unless we are taking a self-defense class, we rarely get the chance to do one-on-one challenges. Of course, we prefer to do it in a friendly way, and that is exactly what this game does.

DIRECTIONS

Pick partners who are about the same size and shape. Have them stand with the length of their sides touching.

Then ask them to press against each other, shoulder to shoulder, trying to make the other person move sideways.

The first one who makes the other move, even a few inches, is declared the winner.

VARIATIONS

Since we all have different strengths, I like to continue this game introducing, each time, a new combat position. Have each pair try them all. They might find that they are weak in the arms, but their butts rule!

Also, try partnering children who are different sizes. Smaller children can be sometimes be stronger than bigger ones.

Hand to Hand

♦ Hand to Hand: Partners face each other and put their arms in front of them, their palms touching. They both push forward and try to push the other person backward.

Back to Back

♦ Back to Back: Partners stand back to back and hook arms. They both try to walk forward, pulling their partner with them.

♦ Butt to Butt and Push: Partners stand back to back and bent over so their rear ends are touching. Each tries to walk backward, pushing her partner forward.

Butt to Butt and Pull

♦ Butt to Butt and Pull: Same as above except when they are bending over, have them reach their arms between their legs and hold each other's hands.

♦ Link Elbows: Partners link elbows and pull to see who can pull whom first.

♦ Hip to Hip: Partners lean away from each other with the top of their bodies and push against each other with their bottom half. Try both sides. See if one side is stronger than the other.

♦ Balance Challenge: Any of the above while standing on one leg.

Hip to Hip

WHAT IS BEING LEARNED

Although a lot of muscle testing and strengthening is going on, when people pit their all against another, a personal connection is created, even if only temporarily. This is because they both intensely shared a moment together. They were in the same physical and mental state at the same time.

It's the reason that often after boys have a physical fight, they're later seen walking with their arms around each other.

ALL AGES

Shoe Mountain

Group
activity

When the kids are bored but antsy with energy, here is a quickie that is guaranteed to win the hearts of all ages. Your twelve-year-old will be just as excited to play this game as your two-year-old.

MATERIALS
shoes

DIRECTIONS
Make a pile of all the shoes you can find in a large cleared space in the room. Tell the kids that this is not a pile of shoes (silly them to think that!), but is actually a huge mountain. They have to start from a distance away and run toward the mountain and then, with one gigantic leap, make it over the top of the mountain to the other side.

It adds to the thrill if the others provide a "drum roll" by slapping their hands on the floor, a table, or their knees as the next leaper makes her run. When that person is in the air, call out her name and applaud when she lands.

VARIATIONS
Hold out a rolled-up newspaper at the end of the run so the players have to end their run by ducking under the roll. This increases their skill because they have to modify their movements to include this change of momentum. Vary the height of the roll so that players have to adjust to different

levels. Announce what you are doing by saying, "This time, I am going to make it even lower!"

Instead of a rolled-up newspaper, you can use a long scarf that is held by two players. This could be the responsibility of a parent and a child who may be feeling too shy or physically unable to play but wants to be a part of the game.

WHAT IS BEING LEARNED

Emotionally, children feel a part of the group when they play this game. During the "drum rolls," they get everyone's attention as they start the run. Then they get the thrill of hearing their name yelled at the height of their victory when they make the jump. Then they receive applause at the end for their success. What could be better?

Socially, they are learning to take turns and that if they wait, their turn will come. Two people can't jump at the same time. If they leap from opposite directions, they'll soon learn that two objects cannot be in the same space at the same time!

Motorically, children are learning how much energy, or "oomph," they need to use in order to leap off the ground. They learn to anticipate at which point in their running stride they need to "take off." Watch children of different ages play this game and you'll see that this is a skill learned through practice. You might see younger learners leaping beside the shoe pile rather than over it as they begin to practice the skill of leaping higher.

Life Is a Kick

One or two
people

Never underestimate the fun of kicking a rock. Many a time, my daughters and I made a long walk shorter by kicking a small rock ahead of us all the way. The person the stone landed nearest to would be the next one to kick it forward.

MATERIALS

something to kick

DIRECTIONS

Play the game described above when walking down an uncrowded side-walk or in the park. If a stone isn't available, there is always something to kick—a fallen acorn, a stray pinecone, even a crumpled-up cigarette pack will work.

See how far each player can kick the object on his turn.

Try kicking with the right and with the left leg to notice which leg is the best at kicking.

Pick a large object ahead, such as a tree or lamppost, and see if the kicker can aim at and hit that object.

VARIATION

A variation on this game can be done at home using a soft gentle object, such as scrunched-up and taped newspaper (see Gentle Ball Games, p. 125, for more ideas). Practice kicking the ball back and forth to one another.

WHAT IS BEING LEARNED

One interpersonal skill is called "shared attention." Developmentally, children go from parallel play, where they each do their own thing next to each other, to the level of attending to the same things.

Kicking a rock together strengthens this skill and promotes teamwork, as well. You share the same goal and take turns reaching it.

This game also encourages eye-foot coordination.

Doodling Doodles

It's fun to doodle, to make little pictures that seem to spontaneously appear when you've got a pencil and a piece of paper and a moment to let your inner creativity come to the surface.

Maybe some evening after the dinner dishes are cleared, your family can play Doodling Doodles. A big part of the fun of this game is making the doodles themselves.

MATERIALS

    paper or index cards
    pens

DIRECTIONS

Give everyone some pieces of paper or index cards and ask them to start by making any doodle that they want. A scribble is fine, an abstract design, a stick figure, whatever comes out. If you want to get more elaborate, use different color pens. Next, each player makes a copy of whatever she doodled on a second card. If there are fewer players, have each player make more doodle pairs.

When the doodle cards are done, lay them out, facedown, on the table, and play the Memory Game.

The first player turns over one card and then another. If the two cards match, she takes them both. If not, she turns them both back over so that they are facedown again.

The next player does the same. As the game continues, players begin to remember where the different doodles are located and can find the matching ones.

The player with the most matches gets to lay the cards out again for the next game.

Very young players can team up with a parent or older sibling.

VARIATION

This game can also be played as a simple matching game between you and your young child. Start with only six doodles and lay them on the table. Give your player the six matching doodles and have her put the matching one on top of the one that is the same.

WHAT IS BEING LEARNED

A simple game requiring only materials made together on the spot can remind us of the satisfying pleasures of human connection.

In this game children are learning to note the details of the doodle they made and using their fine motor skills to purposely duplicate it.

They are also getting a chance to exercise their memory.

Cooperative "Pin the Tail"

Group
activity

This game is something like the old Pin the Tail on the Donkey, except children are trying to complete a drawing of a person. And, unlike the original version, children aren't left blindfolded wandering around the room while the others giggle at their inaccuracy. Instead, they get a little help from their friends.

MATERIALS

crayon or felt-tip marker
large piece of paper (shelf paper, poster board, or butcher paper)
tape
blindfold

DIRECTIONS

Outline a child's body on a large piece of paper. Tape the outline to a wall.

Blindfold each player, in turn, and give him a crayon. His task is to add one part, such as eyes or ears or hair or rings or shoes or whatever, to

the drawing, as requested by the other players. The other players' job is to help the blindfolded person draw the part in the right place by saying things like "more to the right" and "go up" or "you're getting warmer." (You can work out beforehand the type of clues to use.) The next player is then blindfolded and adds another part to the picture. Continue until everyone has had a chance to add a part.

Don't be surprised when the children's directions purposely add the eyes to the kneecaps and put the nose on the neck. Children have a thing for the ridiculous, but the laughter at the result is shared by all, instead of being directed at one person.

VARIATION

The possible variations on this idea are limited only by one's imagination.

WHAT IS BEING LEARNED

Working on a shared project is one way children learn cooperation. In this group game, children get the experience of having a positive result come from listening and following directions as well as giving directions.

Two or more people

A-Step-at-a-Time Toss

I like this variation on the game of catch because children start with success and stay within what I call the "success range." This game gets easier and more challenging depending purely on results.

MATERIALS

"gentle ball," such as a beanbag or crumpled-up newspaper (see Gentle
Ball Games, p. 125, for more ideas)

DIRECTIONS

Starting with two players standing close together, have them toss a gentle
ball back and forth. Every time a successful toss is made, each player takes
a step backward, enlarging the distance between them. If one of them
misses, they each take a step closer, and so on.

VARIATIONS

There are many ways to toss a ball between two partners. Try some of these:

- Toss the ball underhand.
- Toss the ball overhand.
- Both players turn their backs to each other, bend over from the
  waist, and toss or roll the ball back and forth to each other
  through their legs. (This stance is a good way to get fresh oxy-
  genated blood to the brain!)

Older children could try tossing two balls in different ways:

- One person tosses one ball underhand and the other person
  tosses a ball overhand at the same time.
- One person tosses one ball underhand and the other person
  tosses a ball overhand, but the second person waits a beat before
  throwing.
- One person throws both balls so that the other one has to catch a
  ball with each hand.

WHAT IS BEING LEARNED

Children learn the strategy of modifying an activity to include the elements
of success and challenge. They learn to start an activity with what comes
easily and feels successful, then to add enough challenge to sharpen the

skills but not so much as to get discouraged. A-Step-at-a-Time gives children concrete practice doing this together with a partner.

Children also practice eye-hand coordination and learn the necessary skill of anticipating the trajectory of a thrown ball so that they know where to put their hands in order to catch it. Even older children need work on this skill when they are thrown two balls at the same time.

Two or more people

Newspaper Bonnets

If you've got some newspaper and a roll of tape, you can make instant bonnets. I've played this game with children at an orphanage in Cambodia, children at an upscale Montessori school, adults at an Indian reservation, adults at a Micronesian university, and many other places, and I find it crosses all cultures and delights everyone.

One Head Start class made them at Easter time and then paraded around the school showing off their Easter bonnets!

MATERIALS

    newspaper
    tape (regular or masking)
    Optional: decorations, such as paint, sequins, and feathers; and glue

DIRECTIONS

Place one open sheet of newspaper on your child's head. Hold the newspaper to her head by putting tape around the newspaper at the crown of her head.

Scrunch up the paper that sticks out underneath the crown of tape. You can scrunch the paper up in various ways to create different looks. If you roll it up, you get a derby look; if you scrunch it sideways, you get the pirate effect. Experiment with different ways (see illustration).

VARIATION

Don't stop there. Children can make their bonnets unique by decorating them with paint, sequins, feathers, confetti, pom-poms, yarn, or whatever is available.

WHAT IS BEING LEARNED

Children who are having the bonnets made on their heads are learning that if they sit still and don't squirm, something a little amazing will come of it (and isn't that a good thing to know!).

Children who are taping the newspaper onto another child and scrunching up the sides are working with their fine motor finger control and strength.

Children who are decorating their bonnets are practicing their creativity.

Walk This Way

Two or more people

I've played this game with little ones to get them to follow me and go where I wanted them to go. Once at a Head Start outing, the children were running all around and we wanted them to walk back to the school. We started playing Walk This Way, and instead of chaos we had a parade of kids marching, skipping, and waving their arms all the way back to the school.

I've also played this game with sophisticated teenagers who were soon making up fun dance steps to imitate.

DIRECTIONS

Players take turns walking in the front of a line doing whatever movements they want. For example, the lead player can walk like a duck or an elephant or can make up original movements like skipping backward with hands on his hips. Everyone else follows in line imitating that movement.

It's interesting to see how a person's choice of movements often reflects his personality. One person might do a graceful sideways sliding movement while another prefers a snappy forward two-step.

I have found that it's better with little ones (one to four years) for someone older to be the leader, because sometimes younger children can't immediately think of something and the momentum of the game stops. Keep the energy going and moving forward together, and the fun never stops.

VARIATIONS

Have the children stand beside each other instead of behind, and the feeling becomes more like a chorus line than a parade.

Play this game at the beach where each step leaves an imprint in the sand. The players try to step in the leader's footprints. The leader can jump, hop, take big steps or leaps, and the other players can "read" the footprints and follow!

WHAT IS BEING LEARNED

There's a sense of camaraderie and well-being that goes with feeling in sync with everyone else. When children are in rhythm with others, it lessens the feelings of separateness and strengthens the sense of togetherness.

It's also a thrill for them to do a movement and having everyone do what they do. Imitation is still a form of flattery.

Children are also learning the kinesthetic skill of seeing someone else perform a movement and then finding the correct muscles in their bodies to make that same movement.

Bat Square Rhythms

This is a game I learned in New Zealand when I was introducing bat games to a group of Maori. The rolled-up newspaper bats reminded them of a game they play with sticks that involves chanting and timing.

I've since introduced their version at many workshops, encouraging participants to choreograph their own original versions. The variations on this can be endless, so I love to see all the possibilities participants invent.

MATERIALS

    newspaper
    tape

DIRECTIONS

Four players are needed; they sit in the shape of a square with each pair of players facing each other. Each player is holding a bat vertically.

At an agreed-upon count, each player tosses her bat to another person. For example, everyone counts 1-2-3-4 and, on the count of 4, each player tosses the bat to the person on her right. The players repeat this pattern many times, then switch to another pattern.

For example, players can change the pattern to tossing the bat to the person across from them on the count of 3, and so on. There are endless possibilities, such as:

◆ Players use chants or different sounds to indicate the moment to throw.

◆ Players pound their bats on the floor to the beat of the rhythm chosen.

◆ Players throw their bats to the left, or across, or change direction depending on the sounds made.

- Players twirl their bats as they throw them to the other person.
- Players stand or kneel instead of sitting while playing.
- Players tap each other's bats instead of tossing them.
- Attach bells to the bats so they jingle when thrown.

WHAT IS BEING LEARNED

Working with a small group to choreograph a pattern and then having it work out puts people in sync with others, which is a great feeling.

Rhythm and timing are not just musical skills, they are also needed in smooth cursive writing and fluid speech.

Hum a Tune

Two or more people

No matter how patient I think I am, nothing tests me more than waiting in a long line or inching along in snarled traffic.

I found that one way to stay calm and to keep the kids and me amused is to play these quick guessing games.

DIRECTIONS

Take turns humming a tune while the other players try to guess what it is. The player can hum as little or as much of the song as is needed for others to guess. After guessing correctly, everyone can sing the song all the way through or, at least, as many of the words that they can remember!

VARIATIONS

- Say a Phrase: Say the first lines to the song or some phrase from the song instead of humming the tune.
- Write in Air: Each player takes a turn writing a number in the air using a stick or his finger. The other players have to guess what

that number is. The player can have his back to the group or face the group if he is able to draw the number backward. Double- and triple-digit numbers add to the challenge.

♦ Draw in Water: Draw a number or letter in water. Write a word.

WHAT IS BEING LEARNED

These games require concentration as players listen to or look at what another is doing. Any time we get an opportunity to focus our attention, we sharpen our ability to stay in the present moment where learning takes place.

These games also teach children that we can choose how we feel. In this case, we can be irritated by a situation or we can play. The choice is ours.

Who Is This?

Here's a good game to play at any gathering of children who are familiar with each other. I have played it many times at preschools and often amazed the children and the teachers with how well even young children really know each other.

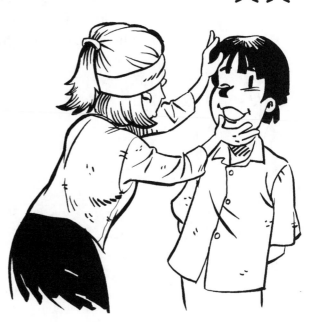

Group
activity

MATERIALS

blindfold

DIRECTIONS

Put a blindfold on the first player.

Once the child's eyes are covered, the group sings this song:

"Who is this, who is this? Can you tell us who this is?"

(I sing it to the tune of the old Campbell's soup commercial. If you're not old enough to remember the Campbell's soup tune or don't know it, make up a tune of your own or just chant the words.)

As the children are singing, I pick a child from the group to come up and stand before the blindfolded child.

The blindfolded child then reaches out and touches the child in front of her. She feels his hair, the contours of his face, and his clothes and then guesses who that person is.

If the player is having a hard time identifying the other (or you're not comfortable with all the touchy-feely stuff), have that person say something and add voice recognition to the game. (With older players, the person can disguise his voice and add to the challenge.)

Once the person is identified, that person becomes the next blindfolded player and the group sings the chant again while you pick the new person to be identified.

WHAT IS BEING LEARNED

Children are becoming aware of details in others, such as hair length and height. They are also developing their ability to "think" with their sense of touch or hearing. They are stimulating their ability to notice the clues that senses other than sight tell them about their world.

Index ~ ~ ~ ~ ~ ~ ~ ~ ~ ~ ~ ~ ~ ~ ~ ~

This index is designed so that you can choose a game by the materials you have handy.

Recyclables include cans, newspapers, plastic bags, and Popsicle sticks.

Household Materials are likely to be found in or around home or school. They include string, rope, blankets, and beans.